THE COMPLETE ILLUSTRATED GUIDE TO
STAMP COLLECTING

EVERYTHING YOU NEED TO KNOW ABOUT THE WORLD'S MOST POPULAR HOBBY AND THE MANY WAYS TO BUILD A COLLECTION

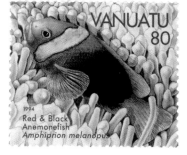

FEATURING EXPERT ADVICE, VIVID EXAMPLES, FAMOUS ISSUES AND OVER 500 STAMPS FROM AROUND THE WORLD

Dr James Mackay

southwater

Author's Dedication: **For my granddaughter, Sophie**

This edition is published by Southwater

Southwater is an imprint of Anness Publishing Ltd
Hermes House, 88–89 Blackfriars Road, London SE1 8HA
tel. 020 7401 2077; fax 020 7633 9499
www.southwaterbooks.com; www.annesspublishing.com

If you like the images in this book and would like to investigate using them for publishing, promotions or advertising, please visit our website www.practicalpictures.com for more information.

UK agent: The Manning Partnership Ltd; tel. 01225 478444;
fax 01225 478440; sales@manning-partnership.co.uk

UK distributor: Grantham Book Services Ltd; tel. 01476 541080;
fax 01476 541061; orders@gbs.tbs-ltd.co.uk

North American agent/distributor: National Book Network;
tel. 301 459 3366; fax 301 429 5746; www.nbnbooks.com

Australian agent/distributor: Pan Macmillan Australia;
tel. 1300 135 113; fax 1300 135 103;
customer.service@macmillan.com.au

New Zealand agent/distributor: David Bateman Ltd;
tel. (09) 415 7664; fax (09) 415 8892

Publisher: Joanna Lorenz
Editorial Director: Helen Sudell
Editors: Catherine Stuart and Elizabeth Woodland
Copy-editor: Beverley Jollands
Designer: Nigel Partridge
Photography: Martyn Milner and Malcolm Craik
Production Controller: Pedro Nelson

ETHICAL TRADING POLICY

NOTE

The stamps reproduced in this book do not appear at their actual size. A small defacing bar has been added to mint issues, where applicable, to indicate that they are a reproduction.

PICTURE ACKNOWLEDGEMENTS

All stamps illustrated in this book and on the jacket were supplied by Dr James Mackay, from his private collection, unless indicated below.
The publisher would like to thank the following organizations and individuals for allowing us to reproduce their pictures in this book:

Key: l=left; r=right; t=top; m=middle; b=bottom

American Philatelic Society: 73tl (all pictures in box), 80 (all pictures), 81br, 82t, 82bl, 84 (all pictures), 86 (all pictures), 89t. Bath Postal Museum: 7tr, 10bl, 12tr, 14bl, 14br, 16bl, 22bl, 23tl, 23bl, 27bl (in box), 42bl (both pictures in box), 50 (all pictures), 52tr (three pictures), 52br (in box), 54tr, 54bl (in box), 55ml and 55bl, 60tl, 60bl, 61tr (in box), 75tl. Arthur H Groten, MD (from his private collection): 57 (all pictures), 64mr (in box). Trevor Lee took the photographs appearing on pages 27tr and 89tr. National Philatelic Society 79br, 81bl, 83bl (in box), 85bl (in box). Philatelic Traders Society Ltd: 83tr. Royal Mail British Stamps © Royal Mail Group plc. All rights reserved. Reproduced with the permission of Royal Mail Group plc. Penny Black and the Penny Black stamp are the registered trade marks of Royal Mail Group plc in the United Kingdom. Anness Publishing Ltd would like to thank Royal Mail Group plc for allowing us to reproduce images of this stamp on the jacket spine and on the following pages: 12t, 13b, 14b, 16bl, 80tr (in box). Royal Mail Heritage: 44bl, 47bl, 72br, 78bl. © Royal Philatelic Society London: 85tr.

The publisher would like to thank:
The Bath Stamp & Coin Shop, 12–13 Pulteney Bridge, Bath BA2 4AY, United Kingdom, for supplying the equipment featuring on pages 28, 29, 30bl, 31ml, 31tr (in box) and 33tr (in box). Linns Stamp News, Sidney, OH 45365, USA for allowing us to reproduce extracts from *Philatelic Forgers: Their Lives and Works* by Varro E. Tyler (1991) on page 60. Stanley Gibbons, 5 Parkside, Christchurch Road, Ringwood, Hampshire BH24 3SH, United Kingdom, for allowing us to reproduce images of their equipment on pages 28, 29 and 30.

The stamps illustrated in pages 1–5 (clockwise from left): p1: Finland, 1982; World Cup, UK 1966; Korea 1994; p3: New Zealand 1940; stamp from tourist set showing fish, Vanuatu 1994; from a diamond-shaped set devoted to indigenous snakes, Guinea 1960s; trams, Hong Kong China 2004; p4: "the new found land", Canada 1947; commemorative stamp honouring hearoes of the Army and Navy, USA 1937; United Nations, USA 1992; Indian paddlng Father Jacques Marquette's canoe, USA 1968; portrait of King Faisal, Saudi Arabia 1964; scenery, China 2004; p5: Christmas stamp, Barbados 2003; Mexico, 1956; Guyana, 1997; Belgium 1995; Laurel and Hardy, 1999 Romania; Germany, 1979.

THE COMPLETE ILLUSTRATED GUIDE TO
STAMP COLLECTING

CONTENTS

INTRODUCING STAMPS AND PHILATELY

Philately, to give stamp collecting its proper name, has been called "the king of hobbies and the hobby of kings" – alluding to the fact that George V and Edward VIII of Britain, Carol of Romania, Alfonso XIII of Spain and Farouk of Egypt were all enthusiasts. The most famous non-royal head of state who was a lifelong philatelist was Franklin Delano Roosevelt. In *The Second World War* Winston Churchill has left a description of President Roosevelt engrossed in his hobby. In May 1943 the two statesmen were staying at Shangri-la, Roosevelt's mountain retreat in Maryland:

> The President had been looking forward to a few hours with his stamp collection. General "Pa" Watson, his personal aide, brought him several large albums and a number of envelopes full of specimens he had long desired. I watched him with much interest and in silence for perhaps half an hour as he stuck them, each in its proper place, and so forgot the cares of State.

All too soon, however, Bedell Smith arrived with an urgent message from Eisenhower. "Sadly F.D.R. left his stamp collection and addressed himself to his task…"

When American GIs entered Hitler's mountain lair at Berchtesgaden in May 1945 one of them retrieved the Führer's stamp album, but it was actually a volume prepared for him for geopolitical reasons, with the stamps of the British Empire arranged to show the Nazi leader the rich prizes that would one day fall into his grasp. There is no evidence that Hitler took a personal interest in stamps, although the Third Reich was quick to harness this medium for propaganda.

WHY COLLECT?

Different people take an interest in collecting stamps for different reasons. Schoolteachers used to encourage the hobby because it stimulated an interest in history and geography, but most collectors are initially attracted by those fascinating little pieces of paper, inscribed in exotic languages, with unfamiliar currencies and views of faraway places. Although stamp collecting is an acquisitive hobby, you do not have to spend any money on it at the outset; the stamps from the letters of friends, relatives and work colleagues will get you off to a flying start.

However, by investing a little more time and money in the hobby, you may soon find yourself on a unique and absorbing journey. In this book we take a look at the various methods of starting a collection and the ways in which it can be developed to suit your own interests and requirements. We discuss the mechanics of collecting, including various tools, equipment, albums and accessories that can greatly enhance the

Above: Definitive sets of mounted stamps are widely available to purchase, and are often favoured by collectors who organize their stamps by country.

systematic development of a collection. You should always remember that stamps are fragile things, originally designed to do no more than perform postal duty once and then be discarded. We look at the best ways to house these delicate treasures so that they are protected from the adverse effects of heat, humidity, sunlight and atmospheric pollution, and how to make sense of their arrangement – chronological or thematic – on the pages of an album.

Left: A 1947 stamp from Monaco showing Roosevelt at his stamp collection. It was designed by Pierre Gandon and does not set a good example for stamp collectors, for its subject is about to scuff the stamps with the cuff of his shirt. It must be presumed that Gandon exercised some artistic licence.

Right: A multi-tiered collectable bearing an Egyptian stamp, a contemporary Army Post stamp and a cancellation made by British field post handstamp E 602 in 1940.

FINDING YOUR NICHE

There are many ways of personalizing a stamp collection. Many collectors begin with a modest idea and then find they lean naturally towards a particular aspect of a country, period or theme. You may enjoy playing the detective, delving into the background of each issue to find out the reasons for the introduction of a change of colour or watermark, why one design was introduced or another hastily scrapped, or why one printer lost the contract and another gained it.

The diligent collector need not limit the search to adhesive stamps. Until the early 20th century collectors indiscriminately took everything associated with the postal service, including stickers and labels, postal stationery and anything that remotely resembled a stamp. These sidelines fell out of favour as stamps became more numerous, but in recent years they have once again become legitimate subjects for study and competitive exhibition. Many of the world's finest collections now encompass much of the ancillary material associated with the production and issue of stamps, from postal notices, leaflets, brochures and other ephemera, to artists' drawings, printers' proofs, colour trials and actual stamps overprinted "SPECIMEN" or endorsed in some other manner to prevent postal use. Add to these items the souvenir folders produced by stamp printers, presentation packs sold by postal administrations, first day covers and souvenir postcards, not to mention the analysis of the stamps themselves, and you will find yourself embarked on a vast and interesting project.

FINANCIAL RETURNS

Every collector dreams of one day stumbling across a cache of ancient letters franked with stamps of immense rarity. Many of the fabulous gems of philately were discovered by ordinary people, even children, and the story of these rare finds and their subsequent history as they advanced in value every time they changed hands

is the very stuff of romance and adventure.

Today, stamp dealing is a global business; thousands of people make a decent living from trading in stamps and no modern postal administration can afford to ignore the revenue accruing from philatelic sales. Philately is one of the few hobbies to offer its followers the opportunity to make a profit at the end of the day. Advice on buying is essential, as are tips on the best methods of disposal and on gauging the value of your stamps, whether solo or part of a larger collection.

The rise of online dealing has taken stamp buying and selling to a new level. All kinds of collectors – from the amateur just starting out to the professional seeking a rarity to complete a prize-winning exhibit – correspond across the globe and undertake bidding wars on international auction sites. Such is the scale of the new e-shopping culture that many philatelic societies now enable members to participate in club trading circuits via email.

GETTING INVOLVED IN THE HOBBY

Philately is highly organized, with clubs and societies at local, regional, national and worldwide levels. Many offer online membership to draw collectors from far and wide, and are an excellent source of information and contacts.

Exhibiting remains a popular objective for the many collectors who like to show off their treasures. The beginner of today, making his or her first display to the local stamp club, may one day aspire to win an international gold medal. This book gives advice on arranging and annotating your collection, and on the

Above: This attractive first flight cover of the Italian Airmail Service, issued on 16 May 1917, bears what is generally recognized as the world's first official airmail stamp. Augmented further by its historic cancellation, this cover has all the elements of a highly collectable piece.

different approaches to displaying material, depending on whether the collection is arranged on traditional lines (by country or period) or topical, or perhaps devoted to telling a story, postal history or sidelines such as air, war or charity issues.

A WORLD OF STAMPS TO CHOOSE FROM

Every country in the modern world has produced stamps at some time. At present there are some 240 countries that issue distinctive stamps, and there are at least three times that number of "dead" countries, which no longer exist as political entities or have changed their name, but which have left their mark in the stamp album.

Below: A historic Madras War Fund charity label produced during World War I to raise funds for a hospital ship.

WHAT ARE STAMPS?

We usually think of postage
stamps as small pieces of
printed, gummed paper, but
in fact stamps, labels and seals
have evolved in response to
various postal functions, and
a wealth of distinctive formats
and affiliated stationery
now exist.

THE ORIGINS OF POSTAL SERVICES

Almost as soon as writing evolved, communications of a sort came into being. Postal services were certainly in existence in China as long ago as 4000 BC and in Egypt and Assyria a millennium later. The Chinese and Egyptian services were confined to imperial court circles, but in Assyria the service was open to the mercantile class as well. Not only are these ancient services well documented in contemporary chronicles, but actual examples of letters have survived, in the form of clay tablets bearing messages written in cuneiform (wedge-shaped) script. An immense hoard of such correspondence was discovered at Kultepe in Turkey in 1925 and included clay tablets dating from at least 2000 BC.

Below and right: Cuneiform writing on a Mesopotamian clay tablet, dating from the 21st or 20th century BC; this was celebrated on an Austrian stamp of 1965 issued for the Vienna International Philatelic Exhibition.

Left: A United States commemorative celebrates the centenary of its country's stamps in 1947.

EARLY POSTAL SERVICES

A regular postal network was established by Cyrus the Great in Persia in about 529 BC, and detailed descriptions of it were written by the Greek historians Herodotus and Xenophon, both of whom commented on the speed and efficiency of the horse relays that carried letters to the furthest reaches of the Persian Empire.

By this time, the Chinese had a highly sophisticated network of post relays. In the 13th century Marco Polo described the imperial service as having over 25,000 relay stations, but as late as 1879 it was still confined to the court, and the general public were barred from using it on pain of death.

The Chinese were also the first to use paper as a writing material, by the 2nd century BC.

Right: A medieval Latin manuscript on another Austrian stamp of the WIPA series of 1965.

The Romans wrote their letters on wax tablets and later on thin sheets of wood, while the Egyptians favoured papyrus. Parchment was the preferred medium in Europe until the 15th century, when paper was introduced from China via Asia Minor and the Byzantine Empire.

By the Middle Ages there were many postal services in Europe, but none was in general use. They operated almost exclusively for trade guilds (such as the Metzger Post of Germany, which served

Above: Postmen from the Middle Ages to more modern times are depicted on stamps of Austria, USA, Belgium and France.

the guild of butchers), the merchants of the Hanseatic League, Venice and the Italian city states, the universities and the great religious houses. When state services were instituted, these gradually died out or were merged with them.

THURN AND TAXIS MONOPOLY

By the 15th century the Holy Roman Empire had an efficient postal service operated by the Counts of Thurn and Taxis, whose range extended from the Baltic to the Adriatic and from Poland to the Straits of Gibraltar. The service survived into the era of adhesive stamps, and issued these in various states of Germany until 1867, when the Thurn and Taxis family (which had backed Austria, the losing side, in the

Seven Weeks' War of the previous year) was forced to give up its postal monopoly to Prussia, receiving 3 million thalers in compensation. The family business had lasted over 420 years, and the last hereditary Grand Master of the Posts died in 1871. (The 500th anniversary of this first great international post was celebrated by a joint issue of stamps in five countries in 1990.)

National postal services evolved from communications established to keep rulers in touch with regional governors. Sometimes a temporary service would be organized to serve the monarch

Below: A Roman cursus publicus *mail coach on an Austrian stamp of 1959, a "ball-wagon" designed to thwart robbers who would fall off after leaping aboard (Denmark, 1951) and the Bath–London mail coach on a British stamp of 1984.*

while campaigning against enemy countries. In Britain, Henry VII had such a service in the late 15th century while fighting in Wales and Ireland. Out of the temporary arrangement set up when Henry VIII went to war against the Scots came the rudiments of the service along the Great North Road. Charles I opened the Royal Mail to the general public in 1635 as a way of raising money without recourse to Parliament (which he had dissolved), and the service was completely overhauled after the Restoration of the monarchy in 1660.

EARLY AMERICAN POSTS

The first postal service in America was established in November 1639, when Richard Fairbanks of Boston became Postmaster to the Massachusetts Bay Colony. Services were organized in Virginia (1657), New York (1672), Connecticut (1674), Philadelphia (1683) and New Hampshire (1683), and were united in 1691 under Thomas Neale as Deputy Postmaster General (under the Postmaster General in London). He was responsible for the handling of all mail arriving from abroad and destined for the various British settlements in North America.

Internal postal services originally radiated from the capital city, but by 1680 cross posts provided a more direct route. The first domestic service was organized by Duncan Campbell of Boston in 1693, operating between there and New York. Other routes, linking Philadelphia to Newport, Virginia (1737) or New York (1742), Boston to Albany, Baltimore to Annapolis and Philadelphia to Pittsburgh, were amalgamated in 1792. The year also saw the first regular exchange of mail between the USA and neighbouring Canada.

CONVEYING MAIL

Mail in the Roman Empire was conveyed by the *cursus publicus* ("public course") using light carts that rattled over paved roads, but the breakdown

A Postal Dynasty

In 1952 Brussels hosted the 13th Postal Union Congress. Belgium marked the occasion with a set of 12 stamps portraying members of the princely family known as the Counts of Thurn and Taxis, who operated an international postal service from 1490 to 1867.

of the infrastructure in the Dark Ages meant that for many centuries most mail was carried by foot or horse posts. This continued well into the 19th century – the term "postmaster" originally meant a horse-hirer. When the age of steam dawned in the 1830s, however, mail by rail began to supersede horses and coaches, just as sailing packets gave way to the first steamships. Although the modes of transport were becoming speedier, the cost of sending or receiving letters remained prohibitively high until 1840, when national postal services underwent revolutionary change.

Left: A US 2c stamp of 1869 showing a Pony Express rider.

Below: A block of four showing historic mail transport, issued for the 20th Congress of the Universal Postal Union in 1989.

BIRTH OF THE ADHESIVE POSTAGE STAMP

On 22 August 1839 the British Treasury was authorized to implement a plan for an affordable postal service, put forward by the reformer Rowland Hill (1795–1874). Seeking inspiration, the Treasury announced a competition for designs and suggestions as to how prepayment of the new Penny Postage might be shown. Prizes of £200 and £100 were offered for the best design and the runner-up. This was widely publicized and eventually drew some 2,700 entries. Although prizes were awarded, none of the winning entries was actually used. One design showing the head of Queen Victoria was submitted by Sir George Mackenzie of Coul, Ross-shire. Recently discovered in the Royal Collection at Buckingham Palace, it is now regarded as the prototype for the first stamp, the Penny Black of May 1840.

Sir Rowland Hill

Born at Kidderminster in 1795, Hill trained as a schoolmaster but also involved himself in social improvements and colonization projects before turning to postal reform in the 1830s. His plan for uniform penny postage was adopted in January 1840, precipitating the use of adhesive stamps.

THE FORERUNNERS OF THE POSTAGE STAMP

All the elements that made up the first stamps were in fact already in existence. Revenue stamps embossed on blue paper had been around since 1694. They were attached to parchment documents by means of lead staples, secured at the back by small rectangular pieces of white paper – the size of the future Penny Black – bearing the crowned royal cipher, and they even had plate numbers and corner letters, just like the early postage stamps.

Newspapers were subject to a tax as a means of raising revenue, often for defence, although they were allowed free transmission by post. It was the extension of this levy to the American colonies in 1765, via the Stamp Act, that helped to trigger the opposition which culminated in the War of Independence a few years later. From 1802 onwards many taxes were denoted by adhesive labels. Indeed the tax stamps applied to patent medicines were not unlike some of the essays submitted in the Treasury competition.

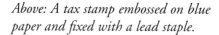

The adhesive labels denoting prepayment of freight charges are thought to have been used by shipping and freight companies

Above: A tax stamp embossed on blue paper and fixed with a lead staple.

Below: An adhesive label used to secure the back of the lead staple (left) and an impressed newspaper tax stamp of the American colonies, 1765 (right).

Above: The first issues of the Penny Black (top left) and Twopence Blue (bottom), as they appeared in May 1840, with an illustration of the crown watermark (top right).

from about 1811, though none is now extant. So the concept of using adhesive stamps to denote prepaid mail was a natural development.

POSTAL REVOLUTION

The Penny Black and Twopence Blue, introduced in May 1840, were a team effort, conceived by Hill, drawn by Henry Corbould from the effigy sculpted by William Wyon for the Guildhall Medal of 1838, engraved by Charles and Frederick Heath and recess-printed by Perkins, Bacon of London. The rose engine used to engrave the background was patented by the American engineer Jacob Perkins, who had devised a method of engraving steel plates to print banknotes that were proof against forgery.

The new-fangled stamps were slow to catch on. At first they were on sale only at stamp offices operated by the Board of Stamps and Taxes, and postmasters had to obtain a licence to sell them. Until 1852 the public had the option to prepay postage in cash, and such letters bore a red postmark to indicate this. Letters could still be sent unpaid, but attracted a double charge of 2d per half ounce.

WORLD FIRSTS

Brazil is generally credited with being the first country to follow Britain's lead, with its celebrated Bull's Eyes of 1843. In fact the New York City Dispatch Post was using 1c stamps portraying George Washington a year earlier. Henry Thomas Windsor, the proprietor of this private local service, was an Englishman who imported the idea from his native country.

The Swiss cantons of Basle, Geneva and Zurich adopted stamps in 1843–5. In 1845 the US Post Office (USPO) authorized postmasters to issue their own stamps, and two years later the first federal issue consisted of 5c and 10c stamps portraying Benjamin Franklin (first Postmaster General of the USA) and George Washington respectively. Every American definitive series from then until 1981 included a representation of Washington, though Franklin was dropped after 1965.

In 1847 Mauritius was the first British colony to adopt adhesive stamps, although Trinidad had a local stamp that year, for mail carried by the *Lady McLeod*, a steamship

Right: Obverse of the 1838 Guildhall Medal, sculpted by William Wyon.

Below: A miniature Isle of Man sheet of 1990, showing the evolution of the Penny Black.

Above: The Brazilian 90 reis stamp of 1843, nicknamed the Bull's Eye.

Below: The first stamps issued for use throughout the USA: the 5c Franklin and 10c Washington of 1847.

run by a private company. Although this showed the ship it was not the first pictorial design to be produced. As early as 1843 the Broadway Penny Post of New York had a stamp showing a steam locomotive.

Bermuda adopted adhesive stamps in 1848, the postmasters of Hamilton (W.B. Perot) and St George's (J.H. Thies) producing them by striking their handstamps on gummed paper.

Above: The 1d Post Office stamp of Mauritius, 1847, and the Bavarian 1 kreuzer, 1849.

Right: The Belgian Epaulettes issue of 1849.

Below: Switzerland's Double Geneva cantonal stamp of 1843, the world's first discount stamp – 5c each or the double for 8c.

In 1849 Bavaria, Belgium and France produced their first stamps and the first decade ended with stamps extending to Austria, Austrian Italy, British Guiana. Hanover, New South Wales, Prussia, Saxony, Schleswig-Holstein, Spain, Switzerland and the Australian state of Victoria. New South Wales had anticipated Britain's adoption of prepaid postage by introducing embossed letter sheets as early as 1838, but adhesive stamps lagged behind by 12 years.

Thereafter, the use of adhesive postage stamps spread rapidly. In 1851 Baden, Canada, Denmark, Hawaii, New Brunswick, Nova Scotia, Sardinia, Trinidad, Tuscany and Württemberg joined the stamp-issuing entities. In 1852 another 11 countries adopted the system, including the Indian district of Scinde (now part of Pakistan), the first country in Asia. With the arrival of the celebrated triangular stamps of the Cape of Good Hope in South Africa in 1853, stamps had spread to every inhabited continent.

ISLE OF MAN 058321

1840·THE PENNY BLACK·1990

Designed by C.Corlett   Printed by Enschede Holland

THE PARTS OF A STAMP

A postage stamp is the sum of many different parts and processes, and two issues that look the same on the surface may in fact conceal subtle variations. An American 32c issue of 1995–7, known to collectors as the Flag Over Porch issue, illustrates this point. To the untrained eye, these stamps look very similar, but their additional features make them really quite different. Although the same printing process (multicolour photogravure) was used throughout, the stamps were produced by four different printers: Avery-Dennison, J.W. Fergusson & Sons, Stamp Venturers, and the Bureau of Engraving and Printing. There are also differences in the gum: some have gum arabic on the back, which has to be moistened, while others have a self-adhesive backing. Some of the stamps were issued with phosphor tagging to assist electronic sorting and cancellation, while others were not. Fortunately the paper was the same throughout and there were no watermarks to contend with, but different qualities of paper and watermarks in many older issues can dramatically affect the value of seemingly similar stamps.

Above: Superficially these 32c Flag Over Porch stamps of the USA are the same, but they were produced by different printers; they are either conventionally gummed or self-adhesive, and are taken from sheets or coils.

PHOSPHOR TAGGING

The 32c Flag Over Porch stamps are all of much the same value, whether in mint (unused) or used condition, but sometimes a very slight variation can make a vast difference to a stamp's worth. Phosphor is used in Britain to distinguish second and first class mail, the stamps having one or two bands, or an all-over coating detected only with an ultraviolet lamp. The British halfpenny stamp of 1971 may be found with two phosphor bands (in sheets) or a single central band (in coils and booklets) and both types are very common. However, in 1972, a prestige booklet in honour of the Wedgwood pottery legacy included a halfpenny stamp in a mixed pane (the term for a page of stamps) with a single phosphor band at the left side only. Today it is catalogued at 100 times the price of the normal versions.

PERFORATION

Rows of holes are punched out of the sheet between the stamps to make them easy to separate, and variations in perforation are the feature that usually distinguishes stamps. Their size and spacing varies, and a gauge is used to measure the number of holes in a length of 2cm/³/₄in. Stamps may be comb-perforated, when three sides are punched at a time, or line-perforated, producing a characteristic ragged effect at the corners.

Before true perforation was perfected in the 1850s, stamps were sometimes rouletted: the paper was pierced by blades on a wheel, but not punched out. This method has survived intermittently to the present day but is more usually confined to postal stationery and stickers. Although perforation is redundant in self-adhesive stamps, it is often retained, in the form of die cuts, for aesthetic reasons.

WATERMARKS

The commonest form of security device, watermarks can usually be detected by holding stamps up to the light. Very few countries now use them, but until the 1970s they were widespread. British stamps of the period 1953–67 may be found with three different watermarks or none at all.

When it is necessary to compare different watermarks a detector is required. The traditional method was

During the first decade of their existence, adhesive stamps were cut, or even torn, from a sheet by the local postmaster. Then, during the 1850s, Henry Archer invented a machine to perforate stamps by punching rows of holes along the white spaces between the stamps to ease separation. This perforating machine (left) is one of the few working Victorian examples left in the world. The Penny Red (above right) issued in 1854, shows a triple perforation – an example of the early teething problems experienced with the new-fangled perforators.

Left: This block of Polish stamps of 1919 was perforated by a comb machine: the regular holes intersect perfectly.

Above: A miniature sheet issued by New Caledonia in 1999 shows reproductions of its first stamp, produced using five different printing processes.

to place the stamp face down on a polished black surface and apply a drop or two of benzine, which momentarily renders the stamp transparent. Nowadays there are various electric devices that are more effective.

PRINTING METHODS

Stamps are printed by a number of different processes, so it's important to recognize their salient characteristics.

The earliest stamps, and most US stamps until the 1970s, were recess-printed from steel or copper plates with the design cut into them (a process sometimes described as intaglio). These can be recognized by the slight ridges (as on a banknote) that result from the paper being forced under great pressure into the recesses of the plate. The opposite process is relief-printing or letterpress, often called typography by philatelists, in which the lines of the design on the plate are raised. Ink is rolled across them and pressed into the paper, producing a smooth surface but often with the design showing through on the back of the stamp.

British low-value stamps were printed by letterpress until 1934, when photogravure was adopted. For this the plate is engraved photographically, allowing fine gradations of tone. When magnified the image can be seen to consist of fine lines due to the screening process. It was first used by Bavaria in 1914 and became popular in the 1930s. In recent years it has given way to multicolour offset lithography, perceived as a cheaper and more reliable process, whereby the image is chemically applied to the printing plate and the ink is "offset" on to a secondary medium, such as a rubber mat, before being transferred to the paper. The image is made up of fine dots.

A few stamps from 1847 onwards were embossed, with the portrait or emblem in relief. Recent attempts to create three-dimensional effects have given rise to laminated-prismatic stamps, stamps in metal foil, images raised by thermography, and holograms.

The Many Lives of a Famous Stamp

1   2   3   4

The Austrian 1s stamp holds the world record for being printed using four different processes at different times. Designed by H. Strohofer to mark the 800th anniversary of Mariazell Basilica, it began life on 22 June 1957 [1], engraved by G. Wimmer and recess-printed (intaglio). On 25 October 1957 it was re-issued as the first denomination in a new definitive series devoted to buildings. This issue [2] was typographed (letterpress), retaining Wimmer's name in the margin. It is similar to the first: the chief differences are the solid value tablet (the intaglio version has criss-cross lines) and the clouds, which are stippled rather than cross-hatched. The rest of the series, as it gradually appeared, was lithographed, and a version of the 1s in this process appeared in January 1959, easily distinguished by the omission of the engraver's name and the lighter colour [3]. Finally a smaller format was adopted for the version of February 1960 printed in photogravure by the British printer Harrison and Sons of High Wycombe [4]. Apart from the Allied occupation set of 1945 (printed in Washington), this was the only Austrian stamp printed outside the country.

STAMPS FOR EVERYDAY USE

In 1840, when the first stamps were issued, there was only one kind, intended to prepay the postage on ordinary letters. When registered mail was introduced a year later, the British Treasury ruled that the 6d fee had to be prepaid in cash, as registration was not classed as a postal service. It was only in the early 20th century, as postage stamps designed to prepay a range of different services became increasingly available, that the permanent issues came to be known as "definitives".

Britain has retained the small upright format of the Penny Black for the vast majority of definitives, and today every denomination, from 1p to £5, is the same size. However, at various times since 1867, larger sizes have been used for the higher values, while the first ¹/₂d stamp, issued in 1870, adopted a small horizontal format, half the size of the 1d stamp. Because most early definitives portrayed a head of state, the upright shape came to be known as the portrait format.

DEFINITIVE SERIES
In establishing a definitive series, most countries followed Britain's lead, although Canada pioneered a horizontal (landscape) format in 1851 for its

Above: One year after the birth of the British penny postage, the Penny Red and "improved" Twopence Blue replaced the original 1840 designs, as part of the Post Office's bid to stamp out postal fraud. While effigies of rulers continue to be adapted or created anew by their designers, the basic format of many "portrait" definitives worldwide remains exactly the same.

Above: Canada issued its first stamp, the Threepenny Beaver, in 1851.

Below: Africa's first stamp: The Cape of Good Hope Triangular of 1853.

Threepenny Beaver, and this shape was later adopted by New Brunswick (1860) and the USA (1869).

The British colonies in North America were innovative in the matter of shape: New Brunswick started with a diamond format in 1851, while Newfoundland's first series (1857) adopted square or triangular shapes as well as a larger portrait size, with a corresponding landscape format from 1865. The Cape Triangular (1853) is said to have been adopted to help semi-literate postal workers sort the mail, though this is unlikely as all Cape stamps up to 1864 were of that shape.

SALE OF DEFINITIVES
British stamps were printed in sheets of 240, so that a row of twelve 1d stamps could be sold for 1s and the full sheet for £1. This pattern was followed in those dominions and colonies that used sterling currency, but elsewhere sheets of 100 or 200 were the norm. In recent years, the tendency has been to produce much smaller sheets, notably in

Above: A portion of a self-adhesive US booklet by Stamp Venturers, 1995–6.

Germany, where sheets of ten are now issued with decorative margins, a marketing ploy to encourage philatelists to collect complete sheets rather than single stamps. In the USA sheets of 20 or 18 are now common.

AMERICAN PORTRAITS
The subject matter of definitive stamps has also broadened considerably in the past half century. From 1847, US policy was to portray dead presidents and politicians and occasionally other historic figures. The series of 1918 revived the landscape format, briefly used in 1869 for $2 and $5 stamps portraying Benjamin Franklin; this was expanded in 1922–5, when all denominations from 20c to $5 used the horizontal shape to show landmarks, scenery and a buffalo to best effect.

The series of 1938 again portrayed dead presidents. The denominations up to 22c portrayed the president of the

Above: Definitive designs: a UK Machin (left) flanked by a Scottish "country" definitive (right).

corresponding number (for example, the 17th president, Andrew Johnson, was shown on the 17c stamp). Most American definitives since 1954 have broadened the scope to include men and women prominent in many different fields.

NATIONAL THEMES

Monarchical countries such as Britain and Spain prefer a uniform series with a single portrait of the ruler. Indeed, the effigy of Elizabeth II, designed by Arnold Machin, has adorned British stamps since 1967 and several hundred different varieties have now been issued. For their low value stamps, the Scandinavian countries and the

Above: Small format definitives issued by St Lucia, 1912 (left) and Sudan, 1921 (right).

Below: Dominica's 1923 series coupled a royal portrait with a colonial emblem.

Postwar German Definitives

The division of Germany after World War II into the Federal Republic, the Democratic Republic and West Berlin resulted in separate issues of stamps in each area. West Germany's definitive stamp designs ranged from the symbolic (posthorns) to presidential portraiture before settling on the themes of technology and famous buildings. West Berlin featured famous Berliners and architecture, while the Democratic Republic favoured socialist celebrities and communist symbolism.

Netherlands have a penchant for designs based on the numerals of value. Norway's Posthorns have been in longest continuous use, since 1871, but Denmark's Wavy Lines are not far behind. Higher values, however, stick to royal portraits. Republics such as France, Switzerland and Portugal prefer allegorical figures.

Above and right: Pictorial definitives from Italy (castles), Austria (religious foundations) and Australia (cartoons).

Below: Historic ships appeared on the Barbados series of 1994–8.

PICTORIAL DESIGNS AND MULTICOLOUR STAMPS

Definitives depicting scenery and the occasional fauna and flora became popular in the late 1890s, beginning with New Zealand, Tonga and Tasmania and spreading to the Latin American countries. By the 1930s the colonies of the British and French empires were indulging in bicoloured pictorials.

The advent of multicolour photogravure, and later offset lithography, broadened the scope in the postwar era, and fully pictorial definitives became the fashion. At first these sets had a mixture of subjects but as the tendency to change sets more frequently has developed, such sets have usually adopted a specific theme, such as birds, flowers, insects or wild animals. Other subjects that have proved very popular include women's costume (Austria), antique furniture (Hungary), coins (Portuguese India) and civic arms (Lithuania).

Definitives are produced in vast quantities – even the Penny Black of 1840–1 ran to some 72 million – but technical alterations during the production, or changes in postal rates, can produce elusive items that soar above their peers in philatelic value.

SHEETS, COILS, BOOKLETS AND STATIONERY

Definitives were always issued in sheets until the 1890s, but other methods of providing stamps have since come into use. In that decade several companies on both sides of the Atlantic devised machines that would dispense stamps. Some were coin-operated but others were intended for use in large company mailrooms, saving staff the time it took to tear up sheets.

COILS AND SHEETS

At first coils of stamps were made up from strips cut from sheets, with parts of the margins used to join one strip to the next; specialists like to collect the coil-join pairs. Later, special printings of stamps from rotary presses produced continuous reels, giving rise to joint line pairs, with a narrow vertical line of colour where the ends of the printing plate met as they were curved round the cylinder. In many countries coils are numbered sequentially on the back of every fifth or tenth stamp in the row.

Apart from the lack of perforations on opposite sides, either vertically or horizontally, coil stamps can be distinguished by their sideways watermark (in Britain) or two or more different stamps side by side to make up the value paid. Similar multivalue coil strips were produced in Britain and later in South Africa in connection with offers made by the *Reader's Digest*.

Left: A US coil of 1912, with private perforations.

Below: A US coil pair of 1983, showing the vertical joint line.

Above: The cover of a British booklet of 1920, advertising Harrods department store.

Right: A Canadian booklet of Flag stamps, 2004.

Sometimes a different theme is used for definitives in coils and sheets. Thus the USA features prominent Americans on sheets and modes of transportation on coils; Germany has portrayed famous women on sheets and landmarks on coils.

Automatic stamps, pioneered by the Frama company of Switzerland in the 1970s, are dispensed by inserting a coin in the slot and using a keypad to tap out the value of the stamp required. The earliest Frama labels were very prosaic, in shades of red ink, but they have become multicoloured and pictorial. Similar systems are operated by Klussendorf (Germany), Creusot (France), Epelsa (Spain) and others.

BOOKLETS AND MINIATURE SHEETS

Booklets of stamps were pioneered by Luxembourg (1895), spread to the USA (1902) and Britain (1908) and are now universal. The stamps are often imperforate on two or more adjoining sides and may be found with inverted watermarks (in Britain) or with different stamps or advertising labels side by side. Originally, booklets were stitched, often with advertising on the covers and interleaves, but in most the panes are now stuck to the cover in a style

developed by Sweden. Britain pioneered the prestige booklet in the 1970s, with mixed panes of definitives as well as combinations of regional stamps or special issues.

Luxembourg also pioneered miniature sheets (1921–3), which have spread around the world. One or more stamps, sometimes forming a large composite design, are set in a decorative margin, with the image on the stamp often projecting out to the edges of the sheet.

POSTAL STATIONERY

These collectables include all kinds of envelopes, letter sheets, postcards and wrappers with some kind of stamp printed on them.

Stamped letter sheets denoting prepayment of postage were in use in Sardinia by 1818. Although the "stamp" actually represented a tax, they were allowed to pass through the post without further charge, so they are often regarded, in Italy at least, as the world's first stamps. Other countries, such as New South Wales (1838),

Below: A composite sheetlet of 12 stamps issued by the United Nations in 1998 for International Year of the Ocean.

Send Money
Securely
by Money
Order
Service

Above: On this Australian booklet pane of 1967, 4c stamps were uprated to 5c.

Russia and Finland (1845) and some German states (1845–8), had similar stamped sheets long before resorting to adhesive stamps. Even Rowland Hill pinned his faith on wrappers and letter sheets designed by his friend William Mulready, issuing adhesive stamps only as an afterthought. The "Mulreadys" gave way to envelopes bearing an

Left and below: Impressed stamps from a 2002 Italian commemorative postcard and a US airmail postcard issued in 1981.

The Mulready Envelope

William Mulready was the designer of Britain's first postal envelope, issued in 1840 but withdrawn in 1841. Its rather pompous decoration, portraying Britannia sending forth her winged messengers to all parts of the far-flung British Empire, inspired a satirical poem in *Punch* magazine and numerous lampoons, resulting in its withdrawal but also triggering off a craze for pictorial stationery.

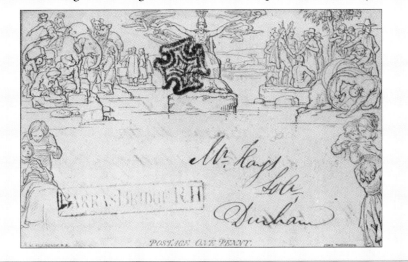

embossed stamp (the Penny Pink, which continued in use until 1902). Special envelopes with crossed blue lines for registered mail were adopted in 1878 and "Official paid" stationery, pioneered by the USA, spread to most countries by the early 1900s. Stamped postcards were invented in Austria in 1869, offering cut-price postage, and spread abroad a year later despite reservations about the messages being read by postal workers and servants.

OTHER STATIONERY

Newspaper wrappers with printed stamps developed in the 1870s. Lettercards – cards folded and sealed along the outer edges by perforated strips that were torn off by the addressee – were first used in Belgium (1882), while Newfoundland (1912) alone produced reply lettercards, with a smaller card inside. Britain briefly flirted with postnotes, folded sheets with an impressed stamp, in 1982. Telegram forms with impressed or embossed stamps were once common.

Special stationery used by government departments has included jury citations and vaccination certificates.

Distinctive stationery for use by armed services or prisoners of war is of particular interest to collectors of military postal history. Austria and prewar Czechoslovakia made enthusiastic use of prestamped postcards for tourist publicity. In Australia, prestamped envelopes and postcards are often employed to commemorate events not deemed to merit adhesive stamp issues.

Since the 1970s there has been a trend towards stationery with a device indicating that postage has been paid, without specifying the amount. Instead the class of postage is expressed, overcoming the need to reprint stationery every time postal rates are increased.

Below: The world's first stamped postcard, issued by Austria in 1869.

COMMEMORATIVE AND SPECIAL ISSUES

The notion that stamps could be used for purposes other than merely to indicate that postage had been paid was slow to catch on. In 1876 the USA produced envelopes with embossed stamps to celebrate the centenary of the Declaration of Independence, but the idea was not adopted for adhesive stamps until the Columbian Exposition in 1893. In the interim, a German local post, the Privat Brief Verkehr of Frankfurt-am-Main, issued a stamp in July 1887 in honour of the Ninth German Federal and Jubilee Shooting Contest. The following year several local posts issued mourning stamps following the deaths of German emperors, William I and his son Frederick III. Many other German local posts had commemorative stamps (including one from Breslau to celebrate the Jewish New Year), but Germany itself did not issue any such stamps until 1919.

FIRST GOVERNMENT ISSUES

In May 1888 New South Wales celebrated the centenary of the colony with a long series captioned "One hundred years". The stamps remained in use for 12 years, undergoing numerous changes in colour, watermark and perforation. Most commemorative issues since that time, however, have been on sale for a short time only, and in some cases from restricted sales outlets. Britain's first adhesive commemorative stamps, for example, publicizing the

Above: The first Mother's Day stamp, released by the USA in 1934, aptly used Whistler's portrait of his mother.

Below: Marshall Islands stamp, 2004.

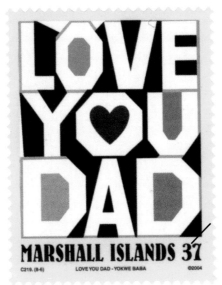

British Empire Exhibition at Wembley in 1924–5, were sold only at the exhibition's post offices.

Commemoratives spread throughout the world. Hong Kong overprinted a stamp in 1891 for the colony's 50th anniversary; El Salvador and Nicaragua issued sets in January 1892 to mark the 400th anniversary of Columbus's arrival in America; Montenegro produced Europe's first commemoratives, overprinting the definitive series in 1893 to mark the quatercentenary of printing; and the Transvaal issued Africa's first commemorative in 1895, to mark the adoption of penny postage.

Not only are commemoratives issued with increasing frequency to honour historic events and personalities, as well

as to publicize current events of national or international importance, but often the subject of the commemoration is used as an opportunity to issue a set of stamps. Thus the maiden voyage of the *Queen Mary 2* in 2004 was the pretext for a set of six stamps depicting famous British ocean liners.

SPECIAL ISSUES

Many postal administrations now augment their definitives with "special issues", a term that covers anything with a restricted lifespan. These issues are generally thematic in nature, often all of the same denomination and increasingly printed side by side in the same sheet. They include stamps for Christmas, Easter, Mother's Day and

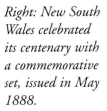

Left: The first adhesive commemorative stamp was issued by Frankfurt-am-Main in July 1887, on the occasion of a shooting contest.

Right: New South Wales celebrated its centenary with a commemorative set, issued in May 1888.

many other such occasions, as well as sheetlets or booklets containing greetings stamps, covering everything from the birth of a baby to "Get well soon" or "I love you, Mom".

STAMPS AND PHILANTHROPY

Philately is the only collecting hobby able to support good causes of all kinds, through the medium of stamps that include a sum payable either to charity in general or to a specific organization. Such stamps are known generally as charity stamps (although in the USA they have been described more accurately as semi-postals, as only part of the charge goes to the postal service).

The concept originated in Britain in 1890, when pictorial envelopes were issued to celebrate the golden jubilee of penny postage. They were sold for 1s but were valid for only 1d postage, the other 11d going to the Rowland Hill Benevolent Fund for Post Office Widows and Orphans.

In 1897–1900 some of the Australian colonies – New South Wales, Queensland and Victoria – issued stamps for Queen Victoria's diamond jubilee or Boer War funds, selling them for 1s, 2s or 2s 6d but providing postal validity for only 1d, 2d or

2½d. The example was followed by Russia and Romania in 1905, but without the outrageously high premiums. These stamps, like the Australians, were issued for specific charities, notably the Russo-Japanese War of 1905, but when the idea spread to other parts of Europe, proceeds were devoted to ongoing good causes, especially child welfare. The stamps issued by Switzerland from 1913 for child welfare, inscribed in Latin "Pro juventute", consisted of short sets, usually with a specific subject. Later this concept was extended to other good causes, bearing the inscription "Pro patria" ("For the fatherland").

WELFARE STAMPS

Germany began issuing welfare stamps (*Wohlfahrtsmarken*) in the 1920s and later added stamps with the inscription "*Weihnachtsmarke*" ("Christmas stamp") or "*Jugendmarke*" ("Youth stamp"). The concept continues to this day. The Netherlands produce stamps inscribed "*Voor het kind*" ("For the child") or "*Sommerzegel*" ("Summer stamp"). Since 1929 New Zealand has issued stamps for children's health camps. Some countries, such as Yugoslavia and Portugal, had charity tax stamps whose use was compulsory

Above: Stamps in aid of the Ludwigshafen explosion disaster in 1948 and New Zealand health camps (1949).

Right: A Netherlands Antilles definitive overprinted for the relief of Dutch flood victims in 1953.

Above: A Belgian charity stamp issued in 1996, illustrating the Museum of Walloon Life.

at certain times, and even issued special postage due labels with which to surcharge mail not bearing the stamps.

Excessive premiums brought charity stamps into disrepute and the actual charity portion is now seldom more than 50 per cent of the postal value. Britain, which started the ball rolling in 1890, did not issue a charity stamp until 1975 (for health and handicap funds), while the USA's first charity stamp (raising money for breast cancer research) appeared in 1988.

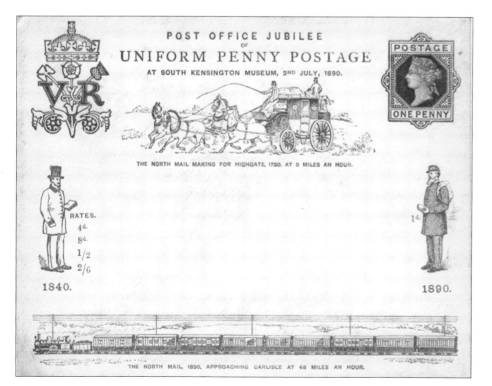

Left: The envelope for the golden jubilee of penny postage contrasted mail communications in 1840 and 1890.

AIRMAILS AND SPECIAL SERVICE STAMPS

Sending messages by air goes back to the 5th century BC, when inscribed arrows were used during the siege of the Corinthian colony of Potidaea. Messages carried by kite date from AD 549 in China, and pigeons have been used since the Siege of Leyden in 1575. The first balloon message was carried by Vincenzo Lunardi in September 1784, and the first official airmail was carried between La Fayette and Crawfordsville, Indiana, by the balloon *Jupiter*, on 17 August 1859.

FIRST AIR MAIL STAMPS
The first regular air service was set up during the sieges of Metz and Paris in the Franco-Prussian War in 1870–1, for which special message forms were inscribed "Par Ballon Monté" ("By

Left: This 1959 US airmail stamp marked the centenary of the Jupiter *balloon flight.*

Below: Loading mail on to the biplane Horatius *at Croydon, south of London, in the early 1930s.*

Above: A French stamp of 1955 showing a balloon flight during the Siege of Paris in 1870.

Right: Private 5c stamp for mail carried by the balloon Buffalo, *1877.*

manned balloon"). Within five years of the first faltering flight by the Wright Brothers in 1903, mail was being flown by plane from Paris to St Nazaire. In 1909 the Peruvian aviator Jorge Chavez carried the first airmail between two countries: Switzerland and Italy.

The first air stamp was a private 5c label produced in 1877 by Professor Samuel King for use on mail carried by his balloon *Buffalo* from Nashville, Tennessee, and showed the balloon in flight. In 1898 1s stamps were issued

in connection with the Original Great Barrier Pigeongram Service in New Zealand. Semi-official stamps for souvenirs flown by heavier-than-air machines at aviation meetings were first issued in 1909 at Bar-sur-Aube, France.

MAIL CARRIED BY AIRCRAFT
India organized the world's first mail service by aircraft (Allahabad to Naini, February 1911), closely followed by Britain, Denmark, Italy and the USA. These services had special postmarks but used ordinary stamps. The USA was the first country to issue a stamp depicting an aircraft, in 1912, but it was part of a parcel post series and had no relevance to airmail. Several other countries featured planes on non-airmail stamps in 1914–15.

Italy produced the first airmail stamp, overprinted for the Rome–Turin service in 1917. The first definitive air stamps were issued by the USA in 1918 and featured the Curtiss Jenny biplane. The 24c with inverted centre was the first airmail error. Thousands of airmail stamps have been issued since, though nowadays many that are specific to airmail rates are no longer thus inscribed.

The Inverted Jenny
The USA released a set of three stamps in 1918 depicting a Curtiss JN-4, popularly known as the Jenny. The 24c was printed with a red frame and a blue centre, but one sheet of 100 was discovered with the centre inverted – one of the greatest American rarities.

Above: Airmails have spawned colourful stationery over the years. As shown by this postcard, it was popular to include illustrations of the planes themselves.

Below: Collectable airmail cigarette cards featured the famous pilots of the day and historic airmail planes.

Colombia, Germany, Mexico and Thailand had lightweight airmail stationery from 1923 onwards, but air letter sheets, or "aerogrammes", were pioneered by Iraq in 1933, followed by Britain (1941) and other countries after World War II. The first British aerogrammes were used for mail sent to prisoners of war and were inscribed in English, French and German.

"BACK OF BOOK" STAMPS

Stamps that were neither definitive nor commemorative but intended for special services have traditionally been tacked on the end of the main listing in stamp catalogues. They are therefore known as "back of book" stamps (BOB for short), a phrase that originated with

American collectors. The largest group are not strictly postage stamps at all, but labels indicating that money has to be recovered from the addressee, either because an item is unpaid or underpaid, or because some special fee (such as customs duty) has to be collected. These are known as postage due labels, although many of them are inscribed "To pay" in the relevant language.

Because they are used internally, few of these stamps bear a country name, and identifying them by their inscriptions or currency is often a headache for inexperienced collectors. Most are quite functional in design, with numerals of value, but more recent issues tend to be pictorial. They were pioneered by France in 1859 and gradually spread around the world.

Stamps for Parcels, Express Delivery and Other Services

Belgium produced the world's first parcel stamps in 1879, but many railway and freight companies had been using them since the 1840s, if not earlier. Britain's only stamps in this category were definitives overprinted from 1883 onwards for use on government parcels. The USPO introduced a parcel service in 1912 and briefly issued a series of red stamps, mainly depicting aspects of postal communications.

Special and express delivery stamps have appeared mainly in Latin American countries but also in Canada and the USA. The latter also issued stamps denoting special handling in 1925–9. Distinctive stamps for registration, sometimes incorporating a serial number, were issued by Canada, Liberia, Montenegro, the USA, Australian states and several Latin American countries.

Official stamps are those provided for the use of government departments. Stamps for separate departments were issued by the USA, Britain, South Australia and Argentina, but elsewhere all-purpose stamps were produced. Definitives were also overprinted or perforated with initials for this purpose. Stamps inscribed or overprinted to

Above: The 1968 US $1 stamp enabled servicemen overseas to send parcels home at a special rate.

Below: Postage due labels from the USA (1879) and Yugoslavia (1948), the latter applied to mail not bearing the compulsory Red Cross charity stamp.

denote a tax on mail during wartime were pioneered by Spain (1874–7) and widely used in World War I.

Stamps have also been produced for many other purposes, such as advice of delivery (Colombia), concessional letters (Italy), journal tax (Austria), late fee (Latin America), lottery or prize draw (Japan and Norway), marine insurance (Netherlands) and newspapers (Austria, New Zealand, USA).

Right: Advice of delivery stamp from Montenegro, 1895.

Below: Parcel postage due label, USA, 1912.

HOW TO COLLECT STAMPS

Armed with a few essential items and some knowledge of stamp care and mounting, the ways you can organize a collection are limitless. Sometimes the choice of what to include seems too great, but, as explained here, there are logical ways to narrow the focus.

STARTING A COLLECTION

There are many different reasons why people take up stamp collecting. A lucky few may inherit a collection from a parent or relative, so they can get off to a flying start and just carry on where the previous owner left off, but most people have to start from scratch. It may be as simple as seeing a particularly eye-catching stamp on an item in your own mail, perhaps from an interesting place you once visited, or depicting a subject that fascinates you, or that is related in some way to your profession or to a school project. The desire to keep it might just be enough to trigger off the notion of forming a stamp collection with a related theme.

We are by nature acquisitive animals, given to collecting items that may serve no utilitarian purpose but which are nonetheless decorative or desirable. As collectable objects, stamps offer variety, rarity, scholarly interest and aesthetic appeal. Ever since the Penny Black first appeared, stamps have been admired and hoarded by collectors for their aesthetic qualities as miniature works of art and masterpieces of engraving, and as exponents of cultural and political ideals.

Above: Pictorial stamps from China and Hungary in 2004 illustrate the popular themes of birds and animals.

PHILATELY TODAY

Not so many years ago most pieces of mail that came into the average household bore adhesive stamps, and it was a relatively easy matter to clip stamps off envelopes. Before long you had the nucleus of a collection, mostly stamps of your own country, but augmented with the occasional foreign stamp culled from holiday postcards or, in some cases, from correspondence sent to the workplace. The chances are that your local town had one or more stamp shops with attractive displays of the world's latest issues in the window to tempt passers-by.

Above: Shops dealing in goods for the stamp collector are fewer than they were, but those remaining are often well stocked and helpful. As they are almost always run by keen philatelists, they are great places to get advice if you are just starting out. Most stamp shops stock starter packs, interesting collections of stamps, and equipment for the specialist.

Adhesive stamps are now virtually confined to social mail such as personal letters and postcards, as most business and "junk" mail bears meter marks or some other indication that postage has been prepaid by a bulk mailer. Meter marks and PPIs (postage paid impressions) do have their own devotees, but they lack the universal appeal of adhesive stamps. Because stamps are now not very plentiful on mail this particular incentive to start a collection, especially among children, may not be so great as it was. However, this does not mean that philately is becoming less popular. On the contrary, postal

Above: An Egyptian "stamp on a stamp", issued in 2004 for the 25th anniversary of the Philatelic Society.

Right: The theme of the Europa stamps in 2004 was holidays, exemplified by this stamp from Guernsey.

Below: Presentation packs, often collected as mementoes by the non-philatelist as well as the keen collector, are an important source of revenue for philatelic bureaux.

administrations all over the world now spend a small fortune on advertising on television and in the press, as well as producing lavish brochures and sales literature promoting an ever-increasing number of special issues and first day covers. The response comes mainly from adults, many of whom may have collected stamps as children and given up the hobby, but returned to it later. Yet philatelic bureaux are also keen to issue stamps bearing themes of interest to

children and young adults, and the prospect of swapping issues with a fellow collector – at a local stamp club or via internet contact – establishes philately as a great interactive pastime.

BE AN INDIVIDUAL
Despite the high-pressure sales tactics, not every newcomer to the hobby slavishly collects the offerings of the national philatelic bureaux. Many start out along that road but quickly tire of following the herd and decide to assert their individuality.

What impels them to continue with stamps may be determined by many other factors. They may be attracted to the stamps of another country because of holidays, military service or business connections there, the latter being particularly useful for continuing and developing the collection. In America, while most philatelists collect US stamps, many are drawn to the country from which their ancestors emigrated. The stamps of Israel and the Vatican are immensely popular with Jews or Roman Catholics for religious reasons. And it may simply be the lure of far-off places that explains the popularity of stamps from places such as Pitcairn and Tristan da Cunha.

These are the main reasons for embarking on a straightforward country collection. You begin with the latest

issues, sign up to a dealer's new issue service or perhaps get your stamps and first day covers direct from the philatelic bureau of your chosen country, and gradually work back in time, filling in the gaps with purchases from dealers or bidding at auction: all these methods are discussed more fully later.

It is often the case that children begin with a general collection, embracing the stamps of the whole world and including anything that looks remotely like a postage stamp. As they grow older and the difficulty of attempting to form a meaningful collection on such a broad scale becomes apparent, collectors gradually narrow their interests and begin to specialize in a single country or even a particular reign or period.

In the past half century, however, other forms of collecting have developed. Paramount is the collecting of stamps according to the subject or purpose of issue, regardless of the country of origin. Others have developed an interest in postmarks and graduated to postal history, studying and collecting cards, covers and other pieces of mail, not primarily for their adhesive stamps but because of their cancellations and other postal markings.

Left: One of a set of 12 issued by the Vatican in 1946, celebrating the 400th anniversary of the Council of Trent.

Below: A stamp promoting tourism for the Pitcairn Islands, 2004.

Every Stamp Tells a Story
Every stamp tells us something about its country of origin, but occasionally the postmark reveals a bigger story. This Irish cover was salvaged from the fire that burned down the Rotunda, Dublin – itself being used as a temporary GPO after the main office was destroyed during the Easter rising of 1916.

TOOLS AND TECHNIQUES

Like any other hobby, stamp collecting requires certain basic essentials, aids and tools. If you buy a starter kit you will find that most, if not all, of these items are included, although as you progress in philately you will probably want to add more advanced versions, as well as other gadgets.

The most obvious necessity is a magnifying glass – the higher the magnification the better. For handling stamps, a pair of tongs or tweezers with

KEY
1 Stamp catalogue
2 Colour key
3 & 4 Perforation gauges
5 Large magnifying glass
6 Sliding stamp magnifier
7 Small plastic tongs
8 Larger metal tongs
9 Small scissors
10 Starter pack of stamps
11 Small magnifier
12 Stamps attached to pieces of envelope.

flattened "spade" ends is a must. To distinguish the subtle differences between stamps you will need a perforation gauge. These range enormously in sophistication (and price), from the basic transparent plastic model with dots or lines to electronic gauges. Similarly, watermark detectors range from a small black tray to machines with lights and filters. An ultraviolet lamp is used to detect different fluorescence and types of phosphor bands.

WHERE TO FIND STAMPS
Sooner or later you are going to be confronted with used stamps in their raw state, still attached to pieces of envelopes or postcards, either clipped off your own mail or purchased in bulk from a dealer who gets his supplies from the various charities that save stamps to raise funds. Banks and mail-order firms are other good sources. You

Above: It is possible to buy world stamps in bulk from a stamp dealer at a relatively low price. Many of these will still be attached to pieces of envelope, or postcards, and will require careful detaching with the aid of a few useful tools before they are mounted.

will find details of the latter in any monthly stamp magazine.

Postal administrations have also got in on the act. In many countries stamps were not affixed to parcels but were

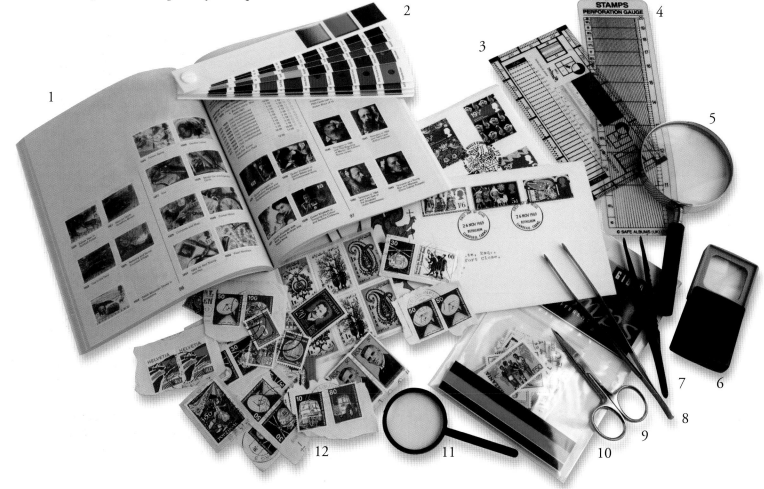

Step-by-Step Soaking Sequence

Perforation Gauge

Invented in the 1860s, a perforation gauge measures the number of holes in a space of 2cm (3/4in). You simply lay the stamp alongside the rows of holes on the gauge until you find the one that fits. This will give you a "perf measurement".

attached to cards that accompanied the parcel to its destination. The cards were then retained by the post office for some time before being scrapped. The stamps, clipped off the cards, eventually found their way into bags sold to dealers and collectors by the kilo – hence the term "kiloware" which is often applied loosely to any mixture of used stamps on paper sold by weight.

DETACHING STAMPS

Once you have sifted through the mixture and selected the stamps you wish to retain, they have to be carefully parted from the envelopes. In the days

Below: When trimming the attached paper around self-adhesive stamps, take care not to damage the perforations, as this detracts from their value.

1. Float the stamps face upwards in a basin or large bowl of lukewarm water. Do not soak them.

2. The stamps will curl away from the paper almost immediately, but you can test this by gently lifting a corner.

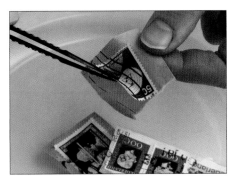

3. Remove the stamps from the water and, with care, use the tweezers to detach from the paper completely.

4. Lay the stamps face down on the top half of a clean sheet of white porous paper to dry.

5. Fold the bottom half of the white paper so that it rests over the top of the stamps, then place the folded sheet between layers of newspaper.

6. Place heavy weights on top and leave for 24 hours before removing the dried stamps and sorting into packets. They are now ready to mount in an album.

when most stamps were recess-printed in monochrome, collectors would quite happily drench them in hot water – but not any more, for modern stamps are printed by less stable multicolour processes on glossy paper with a high chalk content, with fugitive inks and phosphor bands that would be damaged by total immersion. The soaking

procedure described above holds good for the vast majority of self-adhesive stamps, which now have a water-soluble backing. However, some issues from the 1980s, notably from France, the USA and Australia, are backed with a rubber-based adhesive, which defies soaking. All you can do with these is keep them on their paper, trimmed neatly.

HOUSING A COLLECTION

One of the real joys of philately is the satisfaction gained from organizing a motley collection of stamps, covers and postal titbits into a logical, attractive format that can be pored over with pride and interest. Those collectors new to the hobby tend to be familiar with the preprinted fixed-leaf album, where individual spaces for stamps are effectively "drawn" on the page, but there are in fact a wealth of alternative housing options, some of which may not even be designated specifically for stamps. Before purchasing a home for your stamps, you should always reflect upon the type of material you wish to mount: will your collection contain only singles and pairs, or larger items such as First Day Covers and

Below: There are many ways of mounting stamps and stationery for display. Black-backed glassine sheets (left), with clear plastic sleeves already in place, are proving increasingly popular thanks to their user-friendly qualities. To house individual stamps, "Hawid strips" (centre foreground) can be cut to any shape or size, while photo corners (in the red box) are useful for mounting larger pieces of postal stationery. Traditional stamp mounts and pages with a grid pattern offer yet another means of affixing stamps to the page.

miniature sheets? How would you like the material to appear on the page: evenly-spaced individuals affixed using a discreet mount, or slotted into a clear plastic pouch – and against what kind of background? Will you require the flexibility of removing pages later? How much text do you plan to add: a simple label, or a lengthy caption?

CHOOSING AN ALBUM

My very first stamp collector's outfit contained a *Whirlwind* album – small, stapled card covers embellished by a picture of a Spitfire fighter, enclosing pages bearing dotted lines ruled into squares with names of countries and a few illustrations in the headings. A packet of transparent, gummed hinges, a packet of 50 assorted world stamps and the *XLCR Stamp Finder* (a 28-page pocket encyclopedia covering stamps of the world, priced 4d if sold separately) completed the kit that got me started on the right lines.

To this day most albums in starter kits are of the fixed-leaf variety, with printed pages facing each other. They are the most basic and the cheapest, and their chief drawback is their inflex-

Above: Removing the pages from a spring-back album.

Below: Once the pages are removed they lie flat for easier mounting and writing.

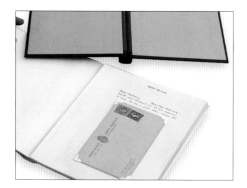

ibility – there is never enough space for the stamps of the more popular countries, while many other pages remain depressingly empty. Also, stamps mounted on facing pages have a habit of catching on each other's perforations if the pages of the album are turned carelessly.

Loose-leaf albums provide the means for expansion and it is advisable to graduate to one of these at the earliest opportunity, once you have decided in which area you wish to specialize. The most basic form is the spring-back type, in which the pages are held firmly in place by powerful springs in the spine. To remove or insert pages, the boards of the binder are folded back to release the spring. This is simple and easy to do, but frequent usage over a period,

Above: Removing a page from an album with a multi-ring binder.

Below: Photo corners are used to mount postcards, covers and miniature sheets.

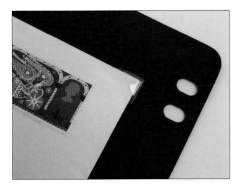

together with the temptation to cram too many pages into the binder, weakens the springs and then the pages are not held as firmly as they should be. The other snag with spring-backs is that it is impossible to lay the pages flat when the album is open.

Peg-fitting albums have the advantage that the pages lie flat, but every time you wish to insert a new page somewhere all the pages before it have to be taken off the pegs and then threaded back on again. This is the system adopted in the most expensive albums, which usually have glassine sheets attached to the front of each page to provide additional protection for the stamps mounted on them.

Less expensive are the albums with a multi-ring fitment. Release the catch and the rings break open so that fresh pages can be inserted wherever you wish without disturbing the others. These albums also lie flat when open. The leaves provided with them have a row of holes punched on the left side to fit the rings. A similar system is used in ring binders intended for holding

A4-size cards slipped into plastic sleeves, and increasingly this type of binder is being adopted by collectors, especially those who prefer to generate their album pages on a computer. For larger pieces of postal material, such as first day covers, clear "photo corners" can be mounted on punched sheets of card to hold them in place on the page.

If you do adopt this system, you must make sure that the cards, if white, do not contain artificial bleaching agents, and that the sleeves are chemically inert, otherwise either may do long-term damage to your stamps.

HINGELESS MOUNTING SYSTEMS

Previously, all stamps, mint or used, were affixed to the page by means of small pieces of transparent paper, gummed on one side. The mount was folded in half and moistened, so that one part adhered to the top of the back of the stamp and the other to the page. The best quality hinges were double gummed so that they peeled off the stamp without damaging it, although some trace of the hinge was inevitable.

In the 1950s, however, a desire for unmounted mint stamps developed in Europe and has now become universal. Dealers encourage this by the wide price differential between unmounted and mounted mint. One solution is to

Hawid Strips

If you are anxious to preserve the value of your mint stamps, you can try the clear- or black-backed mounts known generically as "Hawid strips" (after the German inventor, Hans Widemeyer). The stamps just slot into these, and they certainly enhance the appearance of mint stamps, but unless you are prepared to pay extra for the ready-cut packs they have to be trimmed to size and are fiddly to use.

select mint stamps from the corner of the sheet, with a strip of marginal paper attached, and to affix the hinge to the selvage. Thus the stamp remains unmounted mint, though the page may look untidy as a result.

Below: A stockbook, with transparent strips and clear interleaving, is useful for storing stamps awaiting mounting.

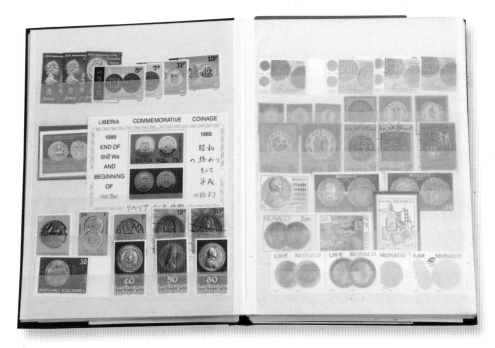

MOUNTING STAMPS FOR DISPLAY

When stamp albums became popular in the 1860s the best of them – fixed-leaf, of course – had printed outlines of the appropriate shape for every postage stamp of the world then known to exist, with the denomination and colour of the stamp in each space. By the 1870s some albums even attempted to illustrate the stamps as well, although the images were often rather crude. The ultimate de luxe albums of the late 19th and early 20th centuries were those with spaces and illustrations on the right-hand page and catalogue descriptions and technical data on the left-hand page. They were sumptuously bound in full morocco leather and fitted with a heavy brass lock.

ONE-COUNTRY ALBUMS

As the number of stamps increased, such albums became less practicable. As late as the 1940s, Minkus of the USA was still offering the "Master Global" album with a space for every stamp since 1840, but this was a philatelic dinosaur and was eventually killed by its sheer bulk. By that time

some publishers, notably Schaubek of Germany, were producing one-country albums along similar lines and this fashion continues to the present day with several companies in America and Europe offering a comprehensive range of such loose-leaf albums, together with annual supplements. The ultimate is

Above: A fast-bound printed album, with stamps mounted on facing pages.

the one-country hingeless album with clear mounting strips already in place over each illustration. The collector with plenty of money but perhaps limited time to devote to the hobby can subscribe to the new issues from a philatelic bureau and merely tip them into the appropriate page.

Although simple, this method is unlikely to appeal to collectors for whom the pleasure of the hobby comes not from acquiring new specimens, but from arranging them, mounting them in albums and annotating them to suit their individual taste. To them, a blank album page, adorned with nothing more than the feint squares that provide a guide to keeping the rows of stamps straight, is a challenge to be faced with enthusiasm. Avoiding the rigid constraints of the printed album, these collectors relish the opportunity to express their individuality, not only by the manner in which they lay out the stamps on the page, but also in the methods adopted to annotate them, demonstrating their technical expertise as well as their calligraphic skills.

Below: An album page showing a World War I cover mounted with photo corners and neatly annotated by hand.

Below: A page of Austrian stamps in hingeless mounts, accompanied by manuscript captions.

Mounting Pairs and Blocks

Multiples can be mounted with hinges if they are in used condition, otherwise Hawid strips can be cut to fit. Provided at least two corners of the block are imperforate, photo corners can be used without blunting the perforations.

Above: A page from a beginner's printed album of the 1950s.

Above: A balanced arrangement of Tuva stamps of different shapes.

LAYING OUT STAMPS

It's a good idea to spread out the stamps you intend to mount on the page and move them around until you achieve a balanced effect. Do not attempt to cram too many stamps on to the page – a common mistake of even experienced collectors. Of course, if you wish to display an entire definitive series you may be constrained by the number of stamps in the set, although the average definitive range

Below: A late 19th-century printed album with a space for each stamp.

consists of about 15–20 stamps. Longer sets, such as the Prominent Americans or Transportation coils, would require two or three pages at least, while the prolific Machin series of Great Britain could fill an entire album.

Try to avoid rows containing the same number of stamps, especially if they are all of the same size and format. Most sets are a mixture of horizontal and vertical formats and stamps for the highest denominations are often larger, but where they are all the same size you can impart some variety by laying out the rows to form a pyramid.

Commemoratives and special issues may present more of a problem, but also offer greater leeway to indulge your artistic skills. Less rather than more should be the keynote. In some cases you may need a row for each stamp, pair or short set, but sometimes you can get two single issues side by side.

ANNOTATING THE PAGES

The number of stamps you can display on a page is also dependent on the amount of annotation you plan to add. The basic data would be the date of issue and the title of the set or stamp. Then you could add the names of the designer and printer and the printing process used. Further information might include details of perforation and watermark, captions for each stamp and even some notes on the reason for the issue, such as additional denominations or changes of colour necessitated by increased postal rates. It is a good idea to map out the text on a scrap sheet to ensure you get the balance right.

If you are annotating the page by hand you should use a fountain pen or a drafting pen, and preferably black ink. Never use a ballpoint pen because the ink may smudge, and pencilled notes will simply fade.

ADVANCED DISPLAY TECHNIQUES

In a stamp album it is permissible to mount appropriate first day covers and souvenir cards. For a more specialized study ancillary material might include original artwork, essays and rejected designs, die and plate proofs and colour trials, as well as covers, cards and wrappers for registered mail and airmail, illustrating the actual usage of the stamps. As well as a straightforward set you would have separate pages for a range of shades, in chronological order of printing, strips and blocks of stamps to show such marginal markings as plate or cylinder numbers, printers'

imprints, alphanumeric controls indicating the year and sequence of printing, or multiples illustrating the exact position of plate flaws and other varieties occurring in the sheet. Information on these topics of interest to the advanced collector will be found towards the end of this section.

The more specialized a collection, the more writing-up is likely to be involved. In extreme cases a single stamp might be mounted on a page with several hundred words of annotation to explain the technical minutiae that make this specimen extraordinary.

INCLUDING POSTAL EPHEMERA

The collectable material associated with the lifespan of a postal service or a particular stamp is often described as "ephemera". For example, a cover or entire letter from the "pre-stamp" era might require all kinds of additional material to illustrate details of the route taken from sender to recipient, the computation of the postal charges and other fees (such as registration or express delivery) and any infringements of the regulations that necessitated a fine or some kind of endorsement in manuscript or by handstamp. Other related ephemera might include press cuttings, photographs or engravings.

The inclusion of collateral material, as it is known, is at the discretion of the individual. At one time, too much of this in relation to the actual piece of mail was frowned on, but it is now positively encouraged and is even regarded as a separate class, known as social philately, in competitions. In this area, considerable ingenuity is required to incorporate bulky and even three-dimensional items, as the notion of philately is stretched to the limit.

Above: A corner of a sheet showing two strips of the Spirit of 76 US stamps, with "Mail early" slogan and Mr Zip.

Below: Plate block of the $5 US definitive of 1975, featuring a railway conductor's lantern.

Right: Picture postcard of the German battle cruiser Derfflinger, *scuttled at Scapa Flow in 1919, with a postcard bearing the ship's postmark.*

Above: Reconstruction of a quarter sheet of New Zealand stamps issued in 1893, displayed to show the advertisements printed on the reverse of the stamps.

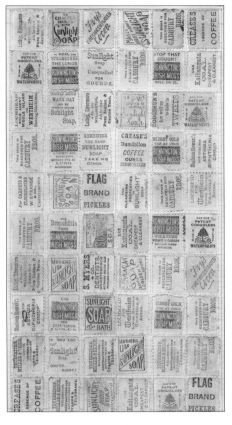

Above: Photographic postcards, such as this issue from St Kilda (1919) showing bales of hand-woven tweed, make eye-catching additions to a stamp display.

Below: This thematic treatment of wartime evacuees includes a billeting permit and a meter mark urging people to "Stay Put!"

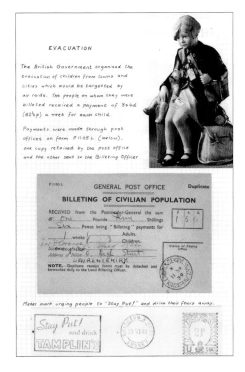

PHILATELY IN THE COMPUTER AGE

At one time the use of a typewriter to produce neat album pages was looked down on, and in competitive exhibitions such entries often lost marks for presentation. In the days of manual typewriters and fixed-sheet albums, the captions and headings had to be typed on sheets of paper, then cut out and pasted to the album pages. The advent of electric typewriters with variable settings and a choice of fonts helped considerably, but now it is a relatively simple matter for the collector to generate album pages on a personal computer and print the results on good quality A4 card, preferably around 160gsm in thickness. Packs of this card cost a fraction of the price of standard album pages and have the advantage that they fit most computer printers; album pages, being generally wider, require a printer with a broader platen.

COMPUTER-AIDED LAYOUTS

The major drawback associated with planning layouts on plain card is that there are no grid lines or "graph paper" squares to guide you in mounting the stamps in neat rows. However, software available for laying out album pages includes a facility enabling you to draw rectangles of varying sizes and shapes.

The requisite captions and other data can then be typed in, using an infinite range of fonts and type sizes, and adding bold or italic variants as required. There is even scope for the use of colour, although you should not get too carried away with this. It is best reserved for bold headings at the tops of pages, but it is also useful for printing the inscriptions on postal markings where the originals are in colours other than black. This makes the text stand out more effectively.

WEB DOWNLOADS AND SOFTWARE

Computers have, of course, many uses apart from generating your own album pages. Collectors are only beginning to wake up to the fact that the search engines on the internet can be used to discover everything you would ever need to know about many of the people and events depicted on stamps.

You can also download all kinds of images germane to your stamp display, such as the actual Old Master painting on which a postage stamp design is based. In some cases there are fees and copyright implications, particularly if you plan to exhibit such material as part of a competitive display, and it does not hurt to enquire about these if you cannot find the relevant information on the site. Many image libraries do not, however, object to the use of

Above: Many word processor documents offer an automatic grid to help you position shapes equidistant from each other: the empty boxes "snap" into place when you drag them into position. While this facility makes for a neat arrangement, it may prevent you from resizing the boxes by delicate amounts to fit the often variable sizes of stamps.

low-resolution digital pictures within a personal collection that will receive limited exposure.

Most importantly, many software packages enable you to create your own catalogue or inventory, complete with regular updates of values, or a database of stamps still required to complete your collection. This field is ever-changing and regular columns in some of the stamp magazines give up-to-date information on such software, as well as a number of websites devoted to helping the collector make the most of the latest information technology.

Collateral Material
Bulkier items, such as this piece of St Kilda tweed, can be mounted in an album or on an exhibition panel by inserting the object in a clear envelope which is itself held in place by photo corners.

COLLECTING BY COUNTRY

Half a century ago there was only one way to collect stamps, and that was according to the country of issue. Within that framework, collectors arranged their stamps by reigns or political periods, in chronological order of issue, and within each issue stamps were laid out in ascending order of face value. Until the 1950s, it was still possible for philatelists to collect stamps on a global basis. In the 1930s the number of stamps issued annually seldom exceeded 1,000, but it began to rise in the 1940s and had doubled by the early 1950s. By 1984 it had risen to over 6,000 stamps a year and today it has risen to almost 15,000. To some extent, this is due to the number of stamp-issuing entities now in existence.

THE GERMAN EXAMPLE
Someone taking all the issues of Germany would, technically, be little more than a general collector of a single country. However, it is a colossal field that encompasses the stamps of 17 states before the formation of the German Empire in 1871, the stamps

Below: The stamps of Hawaii, as listed in The Stamp Collectors' Handbook *(1874), an early stamp catalogue.*

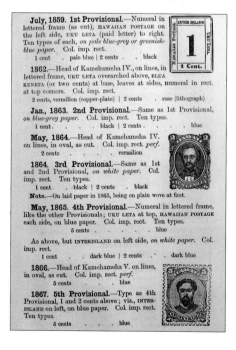

Above: Stamps from Bavaria, the Sudetenland and the French zone of Germany, together with the stamp celebrating German reunification.

of the Reich up to 1945, German occupation of neighbouring territories during the Franco-Prussian War and both World Wars, and all the issues made by the victorious allies when they invaded and occupied the Third Reich. Then there are the stamps of the Democratic and Federal republics (East and West Germany) and the distinctive stamps of West Berlin. The separate issues of the GDR and Berlin ceased when the Berlin Wall came down and Germany was unified in 1990.

Associated with this group are the stamps of the various districts (from Allenstein to Upper Silesia), which, in the aftermath of World War I, were the subject of plebiscites to decide their future. One of these, the Saar, was also the subject of a plebiscite after World War II. Add the stamps of the ten German colonies (1888–1918) and the German post offices in China, Morocco and the Turkish Empire, and you have a formidable body of material. Throw in the private posts that flourished up to 1900 and the emergency local issues, mainly in the Soviet Zone in 1945–6, and you can see the impossibility of tackling this area on anything but a fairly simplified basis.

Above and right: The 5M stamp of 1900, the only German stamp to portray Kaiser Wilhelm II, and a West Berlin pictorial of 1957 which celebrated the 725th anniversary of Spandau.

REGIONAL ISSUES
British stamps are by no means as prolific or complex, but they are difficult enough. Before 1922 there was only one stamp-issuing authority in the British Isles. Today there are nine. The Irish Free State (now the Republic of Ireland) began in 1922. In 1958 regional stamps appeared in Scotland, Wales and Northern Ireland, as well as Guernsey, Jersey and the Isle of Man. England was the last UK country to get

Below, clockwise from top left: Regional stamps issued for England, Scotland, Wales and Northern Ireland.

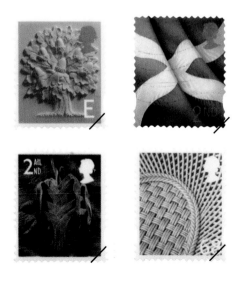

its own definitives, in 2001. Region-alization has also affected other countries. Relative newcomers to the stamp album include the Faroe Islands (Denmark), Åland Islands (Finland), Azores and Madeira (Portugal), the Grenadines, Carriacou and Petite Martinique (Grenada) and Bequia, Mustique, Union Island, Palm Island and the Cays of Tobago (St Vincent).

CHANGING BOUNDARIES

Political upheavals in eastern Europe have seen Czechoslovakia split into the Czech Republic and Slovakia, and Yugoslavia disintegrate into Bosnia and Herzegovina, Croatia, Slovenia, Macedonia, Serbia and Montenegro. There have been separate stamp issues for those parts of Bosnia under the rule of Sarajevo, the Croats and the Serbs respectively. As for the mighty USSR, the solitary issuing authority in 1990 has been superseded by separate stamps for the Russian Federation, Armenia, Azerbaijan, Belarus, Estonia, Georgia, Kazakhstan, Kyrgyzstan, Latvia, Lithuania, Moldova, Tajikistan, Turkmenistan and the Ukraine.

NARROWING THE FIELD

As the number of different stamp-issuing territories has increased, the vol-ume of stamps produced

Right: Portugal issues regional stamps for the Azores and Madeira.

Below: Even Guernsey has regional stamps, for its dependency of Alderney.

Above: Regimes that broke away from the USSR have enjoyed their own stamps. This issue from Kyrgyzstan appeared in 1992, one year after the country's independence.

each year has escalated. Consequently, no one could possibly collect the stamps of the world in the fashion prevalent before World War II.

A surprising number of philatelists do still maintain a general collection, although their criteria have altered over the years. For example, instead of sub-scribing to a new issue service taking all the stamps of the British Common-wealth, they may restrict their interests to used stamps off their mail. This is not such a limited exercise as it might appear for it is interesting to see which stamps actually get used.

Other collectors take the issues of related countries. Interestingly, Irish stamps once had very little appeal to British collectors, partly due to political reasons but mainly on account of the strange script (monastic uncials) and language (Gaelic); but in recent years Irish stamps have tended to stick to English inscriptions and have found favour with collectors who now regard the British Isles as a compact group, large enough to keep them occupied.

The global tendency nowadays is for collectors to focus on the stamps of their own and immediate neighbour-ing countries. Thus American collectors tend to take the issues of Canada, the United Nations, and the former trust territories of the Marshall Islands, Micronesia and Palau. Philatelists in

Ephemeral Nations
Throughout the history of the stamp, governments have used new designs to highlight or stake claims to territory. This *se-tenant* pair of 1993 constitutes the sole issue of Nakhichevan, an autonomous region of Azerbaijan.

Italy concentrate on the prolific issues of San Marino and the Vatican, and French collectors go for the stamps of Andorra and Monaco, and perhaps the country's few remaining overseas colonies in the Pacific, Caribbean and Antarctic.

The natural grouping of countries is often facilitated, indeed encouraged, by the marketing policies of philatelic bureaux, which now tend to handle the issues of neighbouring countries as well as their own. In the People's Republic of China you can buy the stamps of Hong Kong, Taiwan and Macao, and this reciprocal arrangement applies in the "special administrative regions" as well. Thus ordering the stamps of the French group is just as easy as obtain-ing the stamps of France itself and can be done on the same order form or by shopping online.

Below: This stamp of Taiwan (2004), issued by the People's Republic of China, illustrates its scenic splendours.

INTRODUCING THEMATICS

As stamps broke away from the tradition of royal or presidential portraiture, heraldry and allegory at the end of the 19th century and became increasingly pictorial in character, there gradually developed an alternative to the traditional style of collecting stamps by countries. By the 1920s this approach had become sufficiently established for books on stamp collecting to hint at the possibilities of arranging stamps not by their country but according to the subjects they depicted.

THE FIRST SCENIC STAMPS

Pictorial stamps were, of course, issued almost as far back as adhesive postage stamps themselves. The locomotive of the Broadway local post appeared in 1842, the Basle dove in 1845 and the *Lady McLeod* steamship of Trinidad in 1847. British North America and the USA added several stamps with the themes of fauna and transportation between 1851 and 1869, and the earliest scenic stamps appeared a decade later. But these were isolated examples and did not encourage collectors to try a new approach.

PICTORIALS AND PUBLICITY

The period between the two World Wars saw pictorialism in full flood, with the British and French colonial empires and the countries of Latin America leading the field. Ships and trains vied with aircraft as many countries tried to show how modern their communications were. Exotic birds and animals jostled with landmarks and scenery as countries began to realize

the publicity potential of stamps. Newfoundland had been producing pictorial stamps since 1865 but used the diamond jubilee of Queen Victoria in 1897 and the 400th anniversary of British settlement in 1910 as pretexts for long sets publicizing the scenic delights of the colony. From 1923 onwards it produced several definitive sets that were frankly aimed at promoting the growing tourist industry.

In Europe, France was an outstanding exponent of pictorialism, not only in its increasingly numerous commemoratives from 1917 onwards but also in the definitives. Representations of Marianne (symbolizing the triumph

of the French Republic) were favoured for the middle values, but the lowest denominations featured arms of cities and provinces while the higher values since 1929 have depicted monuments and landmarks, beginning with the Arc de Triomphe, Reims Cathedral and Mont-Saint-Michel.

The combination of much more frequent issues of all kinds and multicolour printing processes has widened the scope of stamp design. It is now

Below: Since 1929, many French definitives have depicted scenery and landmarks and could form the basis of collections devoted to specific regions.

Creating a Thematic Display

This page is taken from a collection formed on the theme of the Vikings, who terrorized, then colonized, much of north-western Europe in the 8th–11th centuries. Intrepid seamen and hardy navigators, they discovered Iceland, Greenland and even North America by the year 1000. The collection is broken down into various subjects, such as Norse mythology, metalwork, arms and armour and stone-carving, but their longships could form a separate collection, with stamps from many parts of the world depicting their striped sails and dragon prows. Even ships can be subdivided into river and coastal craft, trading vessels and warships. This collection is mounted on A4 cards with computer-generated headings.

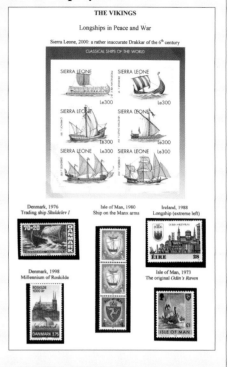

Above: A US $4.40 booklet of 1985 containing stamps showing seashells.

virtually impossible to think of a topic that has not been depicted on a stamp somewhere, at some time. Thematic collecting has liberated philately from the constraints of collecting stamps solely by country.

SUBJECT COLLECTING

The basic idea of thematic collecting is to group stamps according to the subject of the design. When the American Topical Association was formed in 1949 its primary aim was to provide members with checklists of stamps showing different subjects. Today, the ATA has over 50,000 members in almost 100 countries, and has published countless booklets detailing a wide range of different subjects. These have been basic lists enabling collectors to locate the stamps of their chosen subject with the aid of a standard stamp catalogue. However, in recent years major catalogue publishers have begun to produce thematic catalogues, fully illustrated and often in colour.

These catalogues follow a well-trodden path and cover such popular subjects as ships, aircraft, trains, cars,

Below: Chinese and Greek stamps for the railway enthusiast – but you have to look hard to spot the locomotives in the background of the designs.

Above: A Marshall Islands sheet of 50 showing US warships named after each state, from Alabama to Wyoming.

flowers, animals, birds, insects, sports, religion and fine art, as well as such international movements as the Red Cross or the Boy Scouts. There are even catalogues that list all the stamps depicting fungi, seashells and insects such as butterflies, and catalogues that deal exhaustively with ball games or the Olympics. However, many of these categories are broad and it is important to define limits within your chosen subject. It would be impossible to collect every stamp that showed a bird, for example; it makes more sense to focus on individual species that appeal to you, such as robins or puffins.

EUROPA STAMPS

Stamps inscribed "Europa" began to be issued in 1956, and have become one of the mainstays of pictorial subject collecting. Originally, the stamps were confined to the six countries of the European Coal and Steel Community (France, Germany, Italy, Belgium, the Netherlands and Luxembourg). During the 1960s their administration was taken over by the European Conference of Posts and Telecommunications (CEPT), now known as PostEurop, and the scheme has expanded to countries from Greenland to Turkey and the

Ukraine. At first the stamps had identical designs but in the 1970s this gave way to individual interpretations of a common theme.

You can either collect all the stamps with "Europa" in their inscription, or take those Europa stamps that fit the subject you are collecting. In 2004, for example, the theme of the Europa stamps was holidays. Some countries (such as Ireland) opted for tourist attractions such as scenery and landmarks, while others concentrated on sailing, swimming or just lounging on the beach. Many stamps have more than one element in their design. The primary subject will be very obvious, but often there is a secondary subject, perhaps tucked away in the border or the background, and it is the sharp-eyed philatelist who recognizes it who gains points for observation and originality in competitive exhibitions.

Right and below: Stamps from Slovenia, Latvia, the Czech Republic and Greece expound on the holiday theme of the 2004 Europa stamps.

PURPOSE-OF-ISSUE COLLECTING

This branch of thematics, which is also known as incidental philately, deals with the building of a collection around a particular event. A classic example might be a periodical celebration such as an anniversary, but occasionally a single event in history is chosen as a theme.

Anniversaries were among the first of the "global" themes to adorn stamps and labels. The first time stamps were issued in several countries to mark an event occurred in 1892–3, when the United States and several countries of Latin America celebrated the 400th anniversary of the first voyage of Columbus to the New World. In 1897–8 seven countries of the British Empire issued 56 stamps among them to mark Victoria's diamond jubilee; although Britain did not issue stamps, a number of commemorative labels were produced. Around the same period Portugal and its colonies celebrated the exploits of Vasco da Gama. Issues marking the 450th and 500th anniversaries of Columbus, and numerous others on this theme from Spain, Italy and the Western Hemisphere in between, make this one of the largest subjects in this category.

OMNIBUS EDITIONS

Identical commemorative sets issued simultaneously in many territories became fashionable in the French and British Empires in the 1930s. Sets from

Below: A Portuguese stamp of 1894 marked the 400th anniversary of the voyage of Vasco da Gama to India.

numerous colonies and protectorates celebrated the Colonial Exposition in Paris (1931) and the silver jubilee of George V (1935). With uniform designs differing only in the country name and denomination, these set the pattern for many other omnibus issues until the 1970s. Since then, different motifs within an overall uniform style have been preferred. Royalty remains a popular subject, as seen in birthday and jubilee editions and numerous memorial issues for Diana, Princess of Wales.

THE CONQUEST OF SPACE

Space is a vast, global topic with many different strands to be explored, from the Chinese invention of rockets to the Apollo moon landings and beyond, the probes of Mars and Venus and the development of the Hubble telescope. The space race between the USA and the USSR could be illustrated not only

Above: British royal portraiture in stamps has developed enormously, from the restrained, two-colour intaglio pictorials of George V's silver jubilee in 1935 to the multicolour photogravure and offset lithographic stamps of recent years, celebrating Elizabeth II's golden jubilee in 2002 and paying tribute to the Queen Mother following her death.

by stamps but also by souvenir covers and postcards. A straightforward subject collection might consist of the different types of spacecraft, while purpose-of-issue collecting could concentrate on the Apollo 11 mission of 1969 and the stamps that celebrated anniversaries of Neil Armstrong's first "step for mankind", or the issues around the world that mourned the victims of the Columbia and Challenger disasters. The exploration of space might be linked to the devel-

Above: A se-tenant pair – with two designs printed side by side – from the German Democratic Republic, marking the flights of Vostok V and VI in 1963.

opment of the telescope and the science of astronomy. All these aspects now form a distinct branch of the hobby, under the title of astrophilately.

OLYMPIC PHILATELY

In 1896 Greece hosted the first modern Olympic Games and issued a set of 12 stamps, from 1 lepton to 10 drachmae. Although designed, engraved and printed in France, they were wholly Greek in concept. Apart from the 1d and 10d, which depicted the Acropolis and the Parthenon respectively, the designs were derived from ancient Greek sculptures of athletes, or statues symbolizing the spirit of the Games.

Greece produced a second Olympic set in 1906 but this precedent was not followed by any other host

Right: A pre-publicity stamp for the Melbourne Olympic Games of 1956.

Below: A Greek miniature sheet publicizing the Athens Olympic Games, 2004.

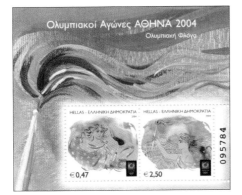

country until 1920, when Belgium issued a set of three, establishing an enduring trend whereby the host nation issues stamps to mark the event. In 1932 the USA became the first country to issue stamps for the Winter Olympics as well. In 1954–5 Australia broke new ground by issuing stamps as advance publicity for the Melbourne Games of 1956. This tradition has now reached the point at which countries begin issuing pre-Games stamps as soon as the winning bid is confirmed.

The Games now include around 30,000 participants, and if you take into account all the stamps marking the anniversaries of national Olympic committees, as well as the stamps and postal stationery provided for the use of the International Olympic Committee in Switzerland, plus souvenir cards and covers, it is not hard to appreciate what a huge subject this has become.

SOCCER STAMPS

If the Olympic Games dominates world sport, the World Cup Football Championship (first held in Uruguay in 1930) is not far behind. Like the Olympics, the World Cup takes place every four years and is now almost as prolific in stamp terms. In the interim, however, the European Cup is beginning to rival the global championships in terms of the outpourings of stamps from participants and non-participants eager for revenue from portraying the great soccer stars. In addition, FIFA, the International Federation of Association Football, celebrated its centenary in 2004 and virtually every affiliated country issued stamps to mark the occasion. There have been stamps for women's football (Nigeria and Sweden), children's soccer (Alderney) and even one-legged football (El Salvador).

Above: This sheetlet from Niger in 2000 was one of a series charting each decade of the 20th century.

Left: One of the stamps issued by Sweden to celebrate the FIFA centenary of 2004 portrayed famous women footballers.

OTHER THEMES

Other aspects of purpose-of-issue collecting are more focused, with worldwide issues for United Nations campaigns, the 75th anniversary and centenary of the Universal Postal Union (UPU) in 1949 and 1974, Rotary International (1955 and 1980), the Millennium (2000–1) and memorial issues for leaders of international renown, such as Franklin D. Roosevelt (1945) and Winston Churchill (1964–5). Many nations brought out iconic stamps to mourn the assassination of President John F. Kennedy in 1963, followed by another set to mark the first anniversary.

The First Olympics

Commemorative stamps were still a novelty in 1896, and a long set with a high face value, as issued by the Greek authorities to mark the Athens Olympics of that year, was roundly condemned at the time. Today, however, the series is highly valued and is the key set for any collection with an Olympic theme.

CHOOSING THEMES AND TELLING STORIES

The third distinct branch of topical collecting offers the greatest scope for the collector's individuality, because it involves selecting and arranging material in such a way that it tells a story. Certain topics in this field are extremely popular because of the range and availability of stamps associated with them.

Raw material for a collection illustrating "The American Dream", for example, is to be found in the definitive sets portraying presidents and other prominent figures, numerous commemoratives or special issues and, in recent years, *se-tenant* strips or entire sheets of different stamps featuring outstanding personalities, from country and western singers to choreographers. More manageable US themes might be "How the West was Won" or "The conflict between North and South." There are also many stamps rather more overt in their promotion and def-

Above: Commemorative and special US issues, usually priced at the domestic letter rate, publicize all aspects of American life. This group highlights youth: the Boy Scouts, Girl Scouts and the National Apprenticeship Program. Even the Automobile Association stamp (1952) stresses the youth angle.

inition of the American way of life, bearing iconic images and inspiring messages to the people of the country.

DIDACTIC STAMPS

Almost from their inception, American stamps have had a didactic element, teaching migrants from many lands something of the customs, history and geography of their adopted land. Stamps "saluted" young Americans with carefully contrived issues highlighting the importance of useful, beneficial activity, such as the Boy and Girl Scouts stamps. The American work ethic was hammered home in numerous celebratory portraits of the blue-collar industrial worker, on issues such as those depicting rail and automobile engineers, postal workers, rangers, apprentices and the country's "future farmers".

In contrast to these, more recent issues address health concerns such as obesity and poor levels of fitness by actively promoting physical exercise. A rather idealized version of the American

Suffragette Mail

A suffragette nails the colours to her mast before a demonstration (left). Some members of the suffragette movement in Britain actively targeted public services, such as the postal network, in a bid to draw attention to their campaign. In some cases, public works buildings were set on fire, while other campaigners resorted to more prosaic, local vandalism to make a point. The envelope below was a victim of such an attack: it was heavily damaged when a suffragette poured ink into the letterbox of an unpopular household.

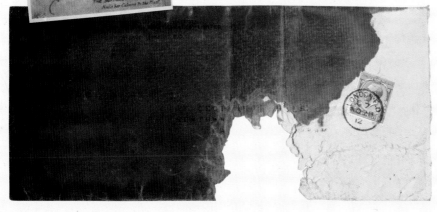

woman as "homemaker" features on several issues, while others champion peace, liberty and diplomacy.

THE TOURIST TRAIL

Another popular approach to creating a narrative collection is to describe a tour around a country, island or even an individual city, illustrating it with appropriate stamps.

Paris and Berlin are excellent subjects for such treatment, because France and Germany (and especially West Berlin when it issued its own stamps) have produced numerous stamps showing everything from panoramic views to individual landmarks. Washington and London might present more of a challenge but it is surprising how many stamps from other countries have portrayed their prominent features. New York City would be much harder. Of course, there are many stamps of the world showing the famous downtown skyline, but only a handful mourned 9/11 with views of the ill-fated Twin Towers. Stamps from many countries marked the New York World's Fairs in 1939 and 1964. The USA issued a stamp in 1953 for the tercentenary of the city, contrasting the Dutch town of New Amsterdam with the modern skyscrapers. New York's Coliseum (1956), University Library (1981), Stock Exchange (1992) and the Brooklyn (1983) and Verrazano Narrows (1964) bridges have all appeared on American stamps, but they are overshadowed by the numerous stamps from the USA and elsewhere featuring the Statue of

Below: Stamps from Nauru in the central Pacific showed solidarity with the USA in the wake of 9/11.

Liberty, an interesting theme in its own right, particularly for collectors concerned with iconography in stamps.

POLITICAL MATTERS

Many countries and regimes have used stamps extensively as political propaganda. Fascist Italy started this trend in the early 1920s but it was taken to new levels by Nazi Germany, and by the countries in the communist bloc when the Cold War was at its height. An interesting collection could be made of the propagandist stamps issued by the former German Democratic Republic, and the means by which it sought to denounce the ideals of the West. From 1940 onwards, the United States has issued many stamps that promote democratic ideals, contrasting the four freedoms enshrined in its constitution with the oppression of the nations then under Nazi occupation or – later – behind the Iron Curtain.

Some stamps, such as those issued by the Isle of Man, vividly illustrate the struggle to win votes for women, featuring portraits of the leaders of the suffrage movement, or the campaigns in many parts of the world to achieve racial equality and civil rights for all. In countries such as Britain, exponents of universal suffrage actually targeted the postal services as part of their national campaign, and remnants of the graphic vandalism exist to this day.

The range of topics with a quasi-political slant is enormous, ranging from the rise and fall of the Roman Empire to the collapse of communism in the 1990s. The French Revolution and its worldwide repercussions and

Above: Many stamps of the GDR commemorated the Nazi death camps, and also portrayed victims of the Holocaust (left).

Below: An American patriotic label from the Cold War era.

the power struggle that led to World War I are themes that lend themselves well to a philatelic treatment.

COLLATERAL MATERIAL

To illustrate a story in real depth, it's important to look beyond the stamps themselves. Increasingly, related material is being brought into play. First day covers (special envelopes bearing stamps cancelled on the first day of issue) and maximum cards (postcards with an appropriate stamp affixed to the picture side, cancelled by a matching postmark) augment mint stamps, but you can also include non-postal labels (sometimes called poster stamps), perhaps commemorating an event or anniversary, or even advertising diverse products in connnection with the event. Pictorial meter marks and postmarks are other items that can be effective in a thematic display.

COLLECTING POSTAL HISTORY

In its broadest sense, postal history encompasses the study of the development of the posts over the centuries. In practice, as a branch of philately, it embraces the collecting of everything pertaining to the transmission of mail, from the cuneiform tablets of ancient Assyria down to the junk mail that popped through your mailbox today. Although postal services of some kind have been around for thousands of years, no one thought of studying the ephemera and artefacts associated with them until the late 19th century – well after the adoption of adhesive stamps and postal stationery.

CANCELLATIONS

The earliest philatelists preferred to collect mint stamps; the cancellation was considered merely to be something that detracted from their appearance. By the 1870s, however, a few collectors were beginning to take note of the cancellations as well as other markings on mail, such as datestamps, charge and explanatory marks, and route and transit marks, which appeared mainly on the backs of the envelopes.

In Britain, some dedicated individuals even travelled round the country trying to persuade postmasters and counter staff to give them impressions of their datestamps, a practice that

Above: An early example of an American machine cancellation, dated 1900, appears adjacent to a 2c George Washington stamp.

Below: "Dumb cancels" (those that do not contain a town or country name) appear in many forms, the impressions often made from shapes cut into cork.

Above: A Pearson Hill parallel motion cancelling machine dating from about 1865.

was regarded in official circles with the gravest suspicion. Although such impressions, on otherwise blank pieces of paper, seem rather childish, had they not been preserved many of the marks would be otherwise unrecorded. The advent of the parcel post in 1883 gave an impetus to postmark collecting, although it was not until 1904 that every post office in the UK was equipped with a datestamp.

Postmark collecting developed around the same time in the United States, where collectors were fascinated by the astonishing range of postmarks.

Above and right: A flag cancellation from Boston in 1898 shows the origin of the seven wavy lines found in machine postmarks everywhere. Such postmarks are immensely popular with American collectors as an adjunct to the many stamps featuring the Stars and Stripes.

It was left to the initiative of each postmaster to devise a mark that suited his fancy, and as well as circles and stars there were numerous pictorial cancellations, cut from pieces of rubber or cork. Around the turn of the 20th century, countless US post offices had

Above: Twin datestamps are typical of the French Daguin cancelling machine.

Below: A dated postmark of Versailles, France, from the pre-stamp era.

machines generating a cancellation whose obliterator took the form of the Stars and Stripes. It is from these "flag cancellations" that the wavy lines in most machine cancellations are derived.

PRESERVING POSTMARKS

The craze for picture postcards from the 1890s to World War I provided an abundance of raw material. Sadly, collectors of the period often cut out the postmark, even cutting into the stamps to achieve a neat little square. This vandalism has destroyed the value of many otherwise rare items. Nowadays collectors keep postcards intact. In the case of ordinary envelopes it is generally sufficient to cut out the stamp and postmark, leaving a generous margin all round. Machine cancellations and slogans are usually kept in strips. Registered, express or other covers subject to special handling, as well as underpaid items surcharged prior to delivery, should be kept whole.

Postmark collecting as a sideline to philately became immensely popular in the period after World War II, when increasing use was made of slogan cancellations that were changed at frequent intervals. Firms would sell the wastepaper from their mailrooms by the sackload for a nominal sum, and this was a fertile source of new material.

Many post offices were still cancelling stamps by hand at that period, but from the 1970s mail was increasingly concentrated and mechanized. Letters and cards are nowadays often transported over long distances to a central automatic processing centre or mechanized letter office, and the cancellations have relatively little relevance to the place where the mail originated. This is true not only of the more industrialized countries such as the USA, Britain, France and Germany, but also of many other countries, which, until quite recently, allowed most post offices to cancel their outgoing mail. It is still possible to get a rubber stamp applied to covers and cards at post office counters in Canada and the USA, but in Britain the only way you can now get a mark distinctive to each office is by tendering a letter or card for posting, and asking for a certificate to confirm this. At one time, a charge was applied for this, but the service is now free.

FROM METER MARKS TO ELECTRONIC POSTAGE

Postage meters were pioneered by Norway and New Zealand in the early 1900s and spread throughout the world from 1922 onwards. Meter marks, which were once despised by philatelists, have become popular in recent years, either as a branch of postal history or as an adjunct of topical collecting (mainly for the pictorial element in their design). Even permit mail markings and postage paid impressions (PPIs), which are extensively used on business mail and bulk mailings, have their devotees: one person's junk mail may be another's collectable material. It is now even possible to download postage through a computer and generate electronic stamps.

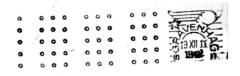

Above: A curious machine cancellation from the Netherlands uses a pattern of dots instead of the usual wavy lines.

Below: Postal history of the future – a postage stamp generated by computer.

Pictorial Meter Marks

From the outset, meter marks offered business users the opportunity to incorporate a slogan showing the company emblem or advertising its products. This also applied to the marks used by offices at local and national government level, and they have often been used to convey road safety or public health messages. Much sought after today are the early meter marks from the United Nations, showing the headquarters building in the "stamp" and the logo and slogans alongside it.

LOCAL PHILATELY

An increasingly popular approach is to concentrate on the philately and postal history of your own town, district, county, state or province. Obviously the various postmarks from your own area will form the core of such a collection, but it is often surprising how much other paraphernalia is available. Some of these categories, such as local stamps of express and parcel companies, private posts, telegraph and telephone stamps, poster stamps and labels, are discussed in more detail later in this section, but by focusing your search for material on a specific locality you will give greater significance to items of this kind.

Above: Stamps issued by three local posts operating in New Zealand, many serving specific regions. Private stamps such as these often yield local markings.

Above and right: Stamps issued by two of the private posts that operated during the protracted British postal strikes of 1962 and 1971.

Left: A parcel stamp issued by the Ardrishaig Mail Service, Scotland, in 1956.

Below: Stamps of the Llechwedd Railway, Wales, with souvenir postmark and cachets, 1980.

WHERE TO BEGIN

You may be lucky enough to live in an area that has made its own distinctive contribution to philately. For example, people living in Oxford or Cambridge, England, could specialize in the stamps and stationery used by the various colleges between 1871 and 1886, when the stamps were deemed to be infringing the monopoly of the Postmaster General and banned. Keble College, which had been the first to issue stamps, celebrated its centenary in 1970 with a souvenir stamp, known on intercollegiate covers. The British postal strikes of 1962 and especially 1971 (when over 200 services briefly flourished) gave rise to private stamp issues in many localities.

In Britain the old railway companies had distinctive newspaper and parcel labels. These were followed by railway letter stamps, sanctioned by the government, from 1891 to 1922, and many of these are of great local interest, especially used on covers with the undated cancellations of local railway stations. On a similar theme, many bus companies had their own parcel stamps, and some still do.

PERFINS

Stamps were sometimes perforated with the initials of organizations as a security measure, to prevent pilferage or misuse. This kind of device, known as a perfin, was adopted in England in

Above: Stamps issued by Keble College, part of Oxford University in England, for the college messenger service in 1871 and 1970.

the 1870s and its use eventually spread around the world. Until recently, stamp collectors tended to regard punctured

Below: Perfins from Argentina and Britain; the latter is a Board of Trade device on a stamp of 1887.

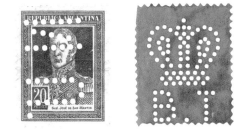

stamps of this kind as imperfect or damaged and either threw them away or ignored them. Then collectors of railway mail realized that the stamps used on company business were invariably perforated with the railway's initials. Since then, serious research has been undertaken in Britain and the USA, where perfins were most actively employed, to identify the companies that used them. Some perfins were used nationwide but most were confined to local businesses and these are now much sought after, especially on covers and cards that have advertising matter printed on them.

LOCAL PO MARKINGS

The collection of local postal markings may encompass every kind of mark, whether handstruck or printed by machine. Naturally, identifying older markings presents the greater challenge to collectors and postal historians.

The earliest datestamps, known as Bishop marks after Henry Bishop, the first British Postmaster General, date from 1660. Originally confined to London, they later spread to Dublin, Edinburgh and some overseas colonies. Dated postmarks did not come into general usage until the early 1800s, but from the 1680s many local offices gradually adopted handstamps that simply bore their name. In some countries, postmarks of the late 18th and early 19th centuries indicated the mileage from the post office to the metropolis.

Below: Records remain of remote or unusual post offices that may no longer exist. Rural England is superbly evoked in this 1937 photograph of Cold Harbour Post Office, Oxfordshire.

Above and right: Pre-stamped jubilee postcard from a German local post (1897) and Scottish postal pioneer James Chalmers on a German local stamp.

After the introduction of adhesive stamps various methods of cancelling them were adopted. Originally it was sufficient to obliterate the stamp with some ornamental device in order to prevent re-use, but by 1844 post offices in the UK had identifying numerals in their obliterators, and this system gradually spread to most other European countries. By the 1850s there were double or duplex stamps combining the obliterator with the office date-stamp, and by the 1880s combined issues had the name, date and obliterator in a compact circular form, a concept that survives to this day.

Small single-circle handstamps were initially developed for telegraphic use in the 1870s, but they have gradually extended to all forms of counter work (registration, parcels and express mail) as well as the agency business that post offices conduct on behalf of other government departments. For all these purposes at least one handstamp (and often many similar stamps) is in use, the postmark distinguishable by a code letter or a number identifying the individual stamper. Separate types of postmark were also used at local level for parcels, registration, or to indicate mail prepaid in cash.

OTHER EPHEMERA

Every postal administration produced an enormous array of stickers and postal service labels. It is important to remember that some of these labels were issued to every post office and bore their own name. In Britain there were parcel (1883–1916) and registration (1907–70) labels personalized to each post office, and a similar system existed in many other countries.

Strike Mail

During the 1971 postal strike in the UK numerous local services operated, complete with distinctive stamps, even switching from pounds, shillings and pence to decimal currency in mid-February. The number of different stamps issued runs to several hundreds.

COLLECTING SEA MAIL

It is little surprise that sea mail is such a popular subject among postal historians, whose collections often include letters, cards and wrappers indicating how mail was conveyed, or bearing evidence of delay or disruption caused by wars and other international upheavals. Some of the best artefacts hint at fascinating stories of global adventure.

PACKET BOATS

Until the middle of the 19th century the chief medium for the conveyance of mail between countries was the sea. In addition, a great deal of mail from one part of the USA to another, or round the British coast, was carried by ship. From the 17th century onwards there were special regulations concerning the transmission of letters by ship. The British Post Office was the world leader in this respect, organizing a fleet of ships, known as packet boats, which operated from Falmouth in Cornwall and carried mail to all parts of the world. Special postmarks bearing the

Below: Ship letter sent from China to Scotland, 1796, via Dover and London.

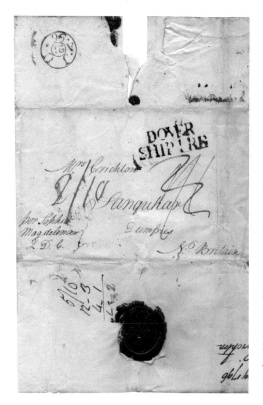

name of the country of posting, with the letter F at the foot in a fancy fleuron, denoted mail arriving in England from foreign parts via Falmouth.

INTERNATIONAL MAIL

Britain established post offices and postal agencies in many countries, enabling people to correspond across the oceans at a time when those countries had barely organized their internal postal services, let alone created an efficient overseas service. Many hundreds of different postmarks evolved in connection with this operation, from departure and transit marks to accountancy marks, showing the postage due in different currencies and often referring to the article or clause in the postal treaty between Britain and the country of posting. Much international mail was conveyed from one country to another on British ships via British ports, so the stamps and postal markings of three different countries might be involved.

SHIP LETTERS

Mail arriving in the British Isles aboard private ships was treated differently. Ships' captains were entitled to a 1d fee on every letter they handed over to the Post Office on arrival and the recipient

Above: A postcard from Spain to London with the Spanish stamps cancelled by the Southampton ship letter datestamp.

paid a ship letter charge of 8d. Special ship letter marks were used by most British seaports – even quite small villages, whose marks are highly desirable.

Many other countries eventually operated similar schemes, but they were consolidated by the Universal Postal Union in 1897 when the French term *paquebot* was adopted. This applied mainly to letters and cards bearing the stamps of one country, posted aboard ships at sea and then landed at a port in another country. Special *paquebot* marks were applied to such mail to explain the use of foreign stamps.

INTERNAL SEABOUND SERVICES

The UK had internal shipping services that regularly conveyed mail and even had shipboard post offices. These operated between Holyhead and Kingstown (now Dun Laoghaire) in Ireland and between Greenock and Ardrishaig in Scotland, and their postmarks are much sought after. Until 1939 cross-Channel steamers had movable mail boxes (*boîtes mobiles*) on deck. They were emptied on the British or French

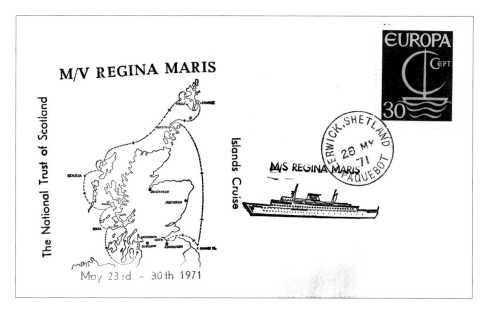

Above: A cover posted aboard the MV Regina Maris *on a National Trust cruise and landed at Lerwick, where the* paquebot *postmark was applied to the German stamp.*

Right: A 25M stamp affixed to a parcel dispatched by commerce submarine from Hamburg to New York in 1916.

Above: A Holyhead paquebot *postmark of 1929 and a backstamp of the Holyhead & Kingstown Packet (1865).*

Below: Paquebot postmarks of 1956 on these Irish stamps were applied at Dun Laoghaire (formerly Kingstown), the Irish terminus of the Irish Sea ferries.

side, and the contents were postmarked at Southampton, London, Le Havre or Saint-Malo, with the initials "MB" or "BM" above the date.

SHIP MARKINGS

Apart from the internationally used *paquebot*, inscriptions on postmarks in many languages provide a clue to their usage in connection with ship mail. You will find *paketboot* (Dutch or Flemish), or perhaps *vapore* (Italian for "steamship"), *buzón vapor* ("steamer box" in Spanish), *Schiffsbrief* (German) or *skibsbrev* (Danish). Less obviously, Australian and New Zealand stamps are cancelled "Loose letter" to denote individual letters brought in by private ships. "Ship mail room" in Australian

postmarks refers to the section of the Melbourne or Sydney sorting offices that processed mail going abroad.

Nowadays many cruise liners have shipboard post offices, complete with pictorial handstamps. The ships that ply along the Norwegian coast between Bergen and Kirkenes each have their own handstamps, indicating the direction, and special postmarks are even applied to mail posted at the North Cape (Nord Kapp).

NAVAL MAIL

Among the most coveted items are those that were conveyed by submarine in wartime. In August 1916, to beat the British blockade, the Germans organized the *Ozeanreederei*, a service to and from the USA using huge submarine freighters, which terminated when America entered the war in 1917; special stamps and cancellations for this purpose were issued by the Deutsche Versicherungsbank. In 1938, during the Spanish Civil War, communications between the Balearic Islands and the Spanish mainland were maintained by submarine and a set of six stamps and a miniature sheet were issued.

Each ship in the German Navy had its own postmark. British naval mail in World War I was marked "Received from H.M. ships", but the inscription "Maritime mail" was substituted in World War II to cover letters from Allied ships as well.

Maiden Voyages

The maiden voyages of mail steamers and latterly cruise liners are often celebrated by special souvenir postcards and covers. These covers from the first eastward voyages of the *Queen Mary*, in 1936, and the *Queen Elizabeth 2*, in 1969, bear US stamps and *paquebot* postmarks.

COLLECTING RAILWAY MAIL

Railway mail forms one of the largest branches of philatelic collecting. Sub-categories include railwayana (where a variety of collateral material might be collected, from rail tickets to the name plates of locomotives) and railroad ephemera, or "railroadia" (popular in the United States), where collectors will try to get their hands on just about anything connected to the history of a railroad route – even lanterns! Various publications and internet auction sites exist for these enthusiasts, but for those who wish to limit their collection to the role played by the "travelling posts" along these rail routes, there is more than enough material to choose from.

Mail was first carried in Britain, unofficially, on 11 November 1830 on the Liverpool and Manchester Railway. The first mail conveyed by rail in America was by the *Best Friend* locomotive of the South Carolina Railroad on 15 January 1831, and by the Baltimore & Ohio Railroad in 1832. The first official mail contract was awarded on 1 January 1838 to the latter company by the US Post Office.

British mail was first carried by train on a semi-official basis on 4 July 1837 by the Grand Trunk Railway, between Birmingham and Liverpool. Frederick Karstadt, the son of a British postal official, suggested that mail handling could be accelerated if it could be sorted en route, and he designed the first sorting carriage – a converted horse-box – which began running between Birmingham and Liverpool on 24 January 1838.

TRAVELLING POST OFFICES
The TPO was the brainchild of Briton Nathaniel Wordsell, who experimented with an apparatus that would allow mail to be picked up or dropped off by

Above: The first purpose-built sorting tender came into use in 1838. The net on the carriage caught the bag of mail suspended at the side of the track.

Below: Postal workers load a travelling post office. The brown overalls guarded against dust and newspaper print.

Above and right: The reason for the delay of this miraculously undamaged American letter would be far from apparent, were it not for the unusual postmark: "Run over by train".

Below: A photograph of a Swedish mail train crash at Rorvik, which occurred on 6 September 1954.

moving trains. His innovation assisted the development of a national rail post network no end, and by 1855 special all-mail trains were running between London and Bristol, and other services spread rapidly across the British Isles in the ensuing decade. A similar pattern developed in all other countries with rail networks during the second half of the 19th century.

THE FIRST POSTMARKS
Distinctive postmarks were evolved for use on mail posted in the special boxes attached to the sides of mail trains or deposited in the late posting boxes at railway stations. In many cases an additional "late fee" was charged, and any items that did not include this were surcharged and fined appropriately. A wide range of explanatory marks also evolved to indicate mail that had been missorted or delayed in transit, while

the rarest, and thus most desirable, marks are those applied to mail damaged as a result of a train crash.

IDENTIFYING INSCRIPTIONS

Special postmarks were devised in every country to denote railway mail. The commonest form was an inscription with two or more names, indicating the termini and perhaps an intermediate station en route. Various initials are another clue, and it is important to spot such designations as "ST" (sorting tender), "SC" (sorting carriage), "RPO" (railway post office) or "TPO" (travelling post office). Inscriptions in other languages may include the words *ambulant* (French), *ambulante* (Portuguese), *ambulancia* (Spanish), *Bahnpost* or *Eisenbahn* (German), *banen* (Danish and Norwegian), *jernbanwagen* (Swedish) or abbreviations such as AMB or EISENB. Some marks used by the old German States were inscribed *"Fahrendes postamt"* (literally "Travelling post office").

Subsidiary inscriptions include "Up" or "Down" in British postmarks, indicating the direction of the mail train, while "Day" or "Night" shows the service. German postmarks often include a numeral preceded by "Zug" or "Z", indicating the identification number assigned to the actual train.

Above: French TPO postmarks can be recognized by their scalloped edge and two place names.

Above: Spanish TPO marks are octagonal, bearing the abbreviation "Amb" for ambulancia *(moving).*

Right: German TPO marks are rectangular or oval, with two names and even a train ("Zug") number.

While the railway postmarks used in Britain, Canada and the USA conform to the patterns for datestamps in general, many European countries have favoured distinctive patterns. Austria, Germany and Czechoslovakia used large horizontal oval shapes, whereas French TPOs traditionally have a scalloped edge. In Spain and Portugal the postmarks are octagonal and the Low Countries use a horizontal rectangle.

WHEN RAILWAY MARKS DO NOT MEAN RAILWAY MAIL

Because of the immense popularity of railway mail, and the premiums paid for covers and cards whose postmarks show that they were carried by rail, it is important not to confuse the railway marks with others that appear to have a rail connection, but do not in fact indicate railway mail.

Many postmarks include words that mean "railway station", such as *Bahnhof* or *Hauptbahnhof* (German), *gare* (French), *stazione* or *ferrovia* (Italian) or *stasjon* (Norwegian). These merely indicate a post office that happens to be located at a railway station,

rather than mail transported by train.

In fact, collecting covers, cards and parcel labels from such station post offices has become quite a study in its own right, but even here some caution has to be exercised. Many country post offices in Scotland included the word "Station" in their name. Of course, the post office may actually have been in the station at one time but in most cases places such as Annbank Station and Drymen Station were villages in their own right. With the closure of many railway lines, the station names have become redundant and the villages have changed their names: these examples are now known respectively as Mossblown and Croftamie.

Below: Many of the preserved railway lines in the UK issue their own stamps, complete with special cancellations and souvenir cachets.

COLLECTING WARTIME MAIL

It is remarkable that even at the height of the worst conflicts, the mail still manages to get through. The Universal Postal Union was the only international organization that continued to operate reasonably smoothly throughout both World Wars, often relying on elaborate routing of mail through neutral countries. Of course, a vast quantity of mail was trapped as the tide of war ebbed and flowed and it was several years before some could be safely delivered.

FPO AND APO POSTMARKS
Special provisions for the handling of letters to and from soldiers and sailors in wartime date from the Napoleonic Wars, and many distinctive postmarks were employed by both sides. The British and French had efficient facilities for the smooth collection and delivery of forces' mail during the Crimean War (1854–6) and from then on special postmarks were employed in virtually every campaign.

A varied, almost chaotic, range of postmarks appeared during the Boer War (1899–1902) but by the outbreak of World War I a system of field post offices (FPO) was in place and this has continued to the present time, with regular numbers identifying the location of units at home and overseas.

Left and below: An Austrian field postmark of 1915 and a letter to Geneva from French troops in Holland during the Napoleonic War.

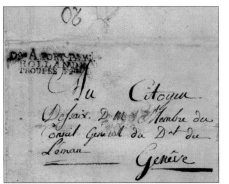

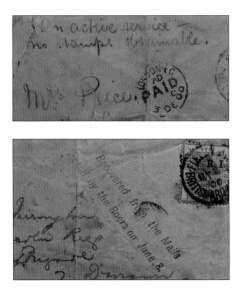

Above: Two APO cancellations dating from 1900 during the Boer War. The scrawl across the top envelope points out that "no stamps [were] obtainable", while the hand stamp below explains that the envelope was "recovered from mails looted by the Boers on June 8".

The transmission of mail to and from soldiers in the American Civil War (1861–5) was often haphazard, but enlivened by a wealth of patriotic covers. A regular service by army post offices (APO) emerged during the Spanish-American War (1898) and was greatly expanded in World War I. The APO system continues today, with numbers identifying offices in Iraq, Afghanistan and other trouble spots.

Below: A stamp postmarked in July 1939 at Camp de Septfonds, a French internment camp for Spanish refugees during the Civil War.

Above: In Britain, the Home Postal Centre in Nottingham was the hub of mail distribution for much of World War II. This clerk is checking a vast index that gave the location of units.

Air raid mail
These two pieces of postal ephemera – a badly damaged newspaper wrapper and a remarkably clean envelope with stamps intact – both survived the carpet-bombing raids targeting southern England in World War II. Note the missile-shaped postmark, applied to wartime mail delayed by enemy action, shown on the bottom envelope.

NAVAL MAIL

Since the mid-19th century a system of special postmarks for military and naval mail has been developed by almost every country around the world. The Franco-German War of 1870–1 and the Pacific War of 1878–83, involving Bolivia, Chile and Peru, yielded a rich crop of military markings, as well as provisional stamps intended for use by the victors in conquered territory.

Naval mail constitutes an enormous area of philately in its own right. While the French and German navies had distinctive datestamps for each warship, the US Navy often resorted to ships' names and other inscriptions set between the obliterating bars of rubber stamps. British vessels, in contrast, retained their anonymity for security reasons. Mail landed from these ships was marked with a handstamp or machine cancellation which read "Received from H.M. Ships". This was altered in World War II to "Post Office Maritime Mail" so as not to exclude deliveries from Allied ships. In World War I each ship was responsible for censoring outgoing mail and a wide variety of marks was employed; these have enabled students to identify many of the individual ships.

Left: Postmark from the German warship Deutschland, *which was interned at Scapa Flow in 1919.*

Below: A World War II cover from England to neutral Switzerland, examined and resealed twice by both British and German censors.

For security reasons, mail landed from warships during World War I was not cancelled by the ordinary postmarks of seaports; instead various dumb cancels were employed on handstamps, in the form of barred circles, concentric circles or crosses. Even cancelling machines had their normal inscriptions replaced by crosses or plus signs. Canada took this concept a step further in World War II, using daters in machine cancellations, devoid of any names or locations.

OCCUPATION, INVASION AND LIBERATION

Occupation stamps were first issued by the German Federal Commissioners in the duchy of Holstein in 1864, following the invasion by Austrian and Prussian forces. It was, incidentally, when the Allies fell out over the administration of the duchies of Schleswig and Holstein that the Seven Weeks' War of 1866 erupted, resulting in many different *Feldpost* markings on both sides. The distinctive stamps for use in occupied territory alone constitute a formidable branch of philately, but the range of covers, postcards and distinctive postmarks is almost infinite.

Special military stationery ranges from the Franco-Prussian and Russo-Turkish wars of the 1870s to the forces' air letter sheets used in Iraq in 2004. Special provision for stamps, stationery and postmarks in connection with the invasion of other countries dates from the 1930s and includes material relating to the Italian invasions of Abyssinia (1936) and Albania (1939), the German invasion of Czechoslovakia (1938–9), Memel, Danzig and Poland (1939), the Hungarian invasion of Slovakia (1938) and Ruthenia (1939). An interesting sideline is the partial erasure of postmarks by the conquerors, cutting out the indigenous version of placenames in bilingual datestamps.

In World War II the Allies made provision for liberation stamps and postal stationery in the aftermath of the landings in Sicily, Italy and Normandy. Stamps were also issued for the Allied

Above: A World War II patriotic cover sent by a soldier in Florida to Canada, transmitted free.

Below: A cover sent from the Cromarty naval base, with the name and date replaced by crosses for security reasons.

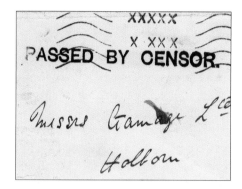

Military Government of Germany in 1945. The stamps of the countries of South-east Asia and the Pacific that were overrun by the Japanese were overprinted following invasion, pending the issuing of distinctive stamps by the occupying power.

SIEGE AND UNDERGROUND POSTS

Distinctive postmarks and cachets are known from various towns under siege, from Paris (1870) to Przemysl (1915); even Mafeking had its own stamps (1900). Underground posts were operated by guerrillas in the Philippines, partisans in Italy and Yugoslavia, and the Boy Scouts during the Warsaw Rising of 1944 (with crude postmarks showing the Scout emblem, carved from half a potato). Internees and prisoners of both World Wars, and even the inmates of the Lodz Ghetto, Theresienstadt and Dachau concentration camp had their own stamps and stationery. Censorship is an enormous subject, with a vast range of re-sealing labels and examiners' marks.

COLLECTING AIRMAIL

The distinctive stamps and stationery devised for mail transported by air has yielded a huge crop of collectable material, and occupies a branch of the hobby known as aerophilately. Yet it is the vast history of the service itself, spanning some two centuries, that often prompts collectors to take a closer interest in this field. Behind the postmarked envelopes and first flight covers are fascinating accounts of some of the most daring, innovative and bizarre methods of carrying mail ever devised.

Left and above: A Swiss stamp celebrating the first round-the-world balloon flight (1999), and the launch of balloons during the Siege of Paris (1870–1).

Right and below right: The Graf Zeppelin moored at Los Angeles on 26 August 1929, following a 79-hour Pacific crossing, and one of three US stamps issued to celebrate its Europe–Pan-American flight in 1930.

BALLOON POSTS

It was not long after the first hot-air balloon flights by the Montgolfier brothers in France and Vincenzo Lunardi in Britain that attempts were made to carry mail by balloon. In 1807 during the Peninsular War, propaganda leaflets were dropped over the French lines, and thus began a branch of postal history known as "psywar" (psychological warfare) that is of immense interest to airmail buffs as well as military postal historians.

The first commercial balloon posts were organized during the sieges of Metz and Paris in 1870–1. Of the 65 balloons flown out of Paris, six were captured by the enemy, two were blown out to sea and never seen again and the others made safe landings and delivered their precious cargo of letters. These balloons came down all over the place, including one that landed at Lifjeld in Norway, having flown 3,142km/1,952 miles in 14 hours: its record airspeed of 241kph/150mph was not broken until 1915.

Unmanned free balloons were occasionally used to transmit mail during World War I but in the interwar period they were mainly associated with the souvenir mail carried by contestants in the Gordon Bennett balloon races (for which special stamps were also issued). The trouble with free balloons was that they went wherever the wind blew and it was only in 1999 that a balloon capable of reaching the steady airstream in the upper atmosphere could circumnavigate the world, a feat celebrated by a special cover from Switzerland.

Experiments with dirigible balloons by Santos Dumont in Brazil and Count Ferdinand von Zeppelin in Germany led to the airships of World War I and the giant zeppelins of the 1920s and 1930s, which achieved epic transatlantic, polar and global journeys. Zeppelin mail has a large number of devotees, and items include the charred covers from the ill-fated *Hindenburg*, which crashed in New Jersey, in 1937.

The Birth of the US Airmail Service

In 1918, the US Army was persuaded to lend pilots and planes to establish air routes for mail delivery. Within a few years, the service was a thriving commercial enterprise, with airlines dispatching mail at affordable rates.

Above: A souvenir cover from the first night mail flight between Sweden and Croydon, England, in 1928.

HEAVIER-THAN-AIR MACHINES

Within five years of the first flight by the Wright Brothers in 1903, mail was being carried by aircraft in France. Sir Walter Windham, a British pioneer of aviation, organized the first official airmail between Allahabad and Naini, India, in February 1911 and swiftly followed this with the Coronation Aerial Post between London and Windsor in September. Denmark, Italy and the USA all had official airmails launched in the same month.

Mail flown over sea between two countries began with Augustin Parla's flight of July 1913 between Florida and Cuba, and this was followed by the

Above: A cigarette card featuring an "Empire" class flying boat.

Below: US Postmaster James A. Farley helps to stack mail delivered from a flying boat on 22 November 1935.

Above: A first flight cover from the gold-mining town of Herb Lake to The Pas in Manitoba, Canada, 1937.

flight of January 1914 between Buenos Aires and Montevideo by Teodoro Fels. Five years later John Alcock and Arthur Whitten-Brown made the first successful non-stop crossing of the Atlantic, flying from St John's, Newfoundland to Clifden, County Galway, Ireland. Ironically, the postal covers that were salvaged from the wrecks of the earlier, unsuccessful competitors in this endeavour now rate much more highly than those from the successful flight.

The heyday of pioneer airmails was the 1920s, when many countries made their first attempts to organize air routes, and the postal subsidies were a major factor in their success. Large countries such as Canada, Australia, Brazil and the USA were in the forefront of this development. In addition to first flight covers with colourful cachets and postmarks, airport dedication souvenirs were produced, notably in the USA where local airports proliferated in this period.

In the 1930s the great transoceanic air routes became commercially feasible, and their development was duly charted by the special covers and postcards associated with the Clipper flying boats. There were also ingenious attempts by France and Germany to accelerate sea mail by using small aircraft catapulted from the decks of ocean liners as they drew near to land. In 1928 France even issued special stamps for this service operated by the liner *Ile de France,* while the catapult mail from the German ships *Bremen* and *Europa* (1929) was marked with distinctive cachets.

HELICOPTER MAIL

Conventional aircraft required a lengthy runway, but the problem of short take-off and landing was solved by the development of the autogiro in the 1930s. Souvenir covers associated with this short-lived aircraft are known from England, Spain, Australia, Canada and the USA between 1934 and 1939. The autogiro was eclipsed by the helicopter, which was developed during World War II and first used to carry mail at Los Angeles in July 1946. At first helicopter flights were confined to emergencies, but in the UK regular commercial mail services were inaugurated in East Anglia in June 1948.

FROM PIGEONGRAMS TO ROCKET MAIL

Carrier pigeons have been used to convey urgent messages since the days of ancient Greece, but the first regular commercial service was organized during the Siege of Paris in 1870–1. More than 300 birds flew messages into the beleaguered city. At first, handwritten flimsies were attached to them but later microfilm *pellicules* were used. The pigeons were taken out of Paris aboard manned balloons. Pigeongrams were widely used in New Zealand from 1896 and in India from 1931 to 1941.

Mail-carrying rockets were devised in Austria and Germany in 1928–31 and were used extensively in India between 1934 and 1944, while Cuba even issued a special stamp for a rocket mail service in 1939.

Below: A cover from the first official helicopter mail flight, from Lowestoft to Peterborough, in 1948.

CINDERELLA PHILATELY

Everyone is familiar with the story of Cinderella, neglected and mistreated by her ugly stepsisters, but transformed by her fairy godmother into the belle of the ball. The parallel between Cinderella and the byways of philately is close, and it is appropriate that the sidelines of the hobby, once despised and ignored, have now developed a strong following and, in fact, form a major branch of philately with its own societies. Many of these have websites where members discuss literature on the subject, specialized auctions and insuring expensive collectables. A list of useful addresses for the aspiring Cinderella philatelist is included at the end of this book.

ALBUM WEEDS
Back in the 19th century, when stamp collecting was still in its infancy, collectors did not have at their disposal a

Right: The £5 stamp used on British Army telegraphs, and a Victorian label for securing the lead seal on the tax stamps affixed to legal documents.

Below: A page from Collecting Postage Stamps *by L.N. & M. Williams (1950), giving examples of "what not to collect".*

wealth of handbooks and monographs, let alone the priced catalogues that are now easily available, or the infinite mass of data on the internet. They therefore operated on the principle of "if it looks like a stamp, stick it in the album". Among these were forgeries and utterly bogus issues, produced solely to defraud collectors. The Reverend R.B. Earee coined the term "album weeds" in the 1870s and such fabrications were the first to go, but many years later philatelists realized that it was important to study forgeries, if only to help collectors distinguish between the genuine and the false.

The brothers Norman and Maurice Williams wrote many books on philately from the 1930s to the 1970s. In one of them, aimed at youthful beginners, they illustrated a range of stamp-like objects – labels, fiscals, telegraph stamps, Christmas seals and the

Above: A Frama label (automatic machine stamp) issued by New Zealand.

Right: A self-adhesive service indicator label used at British post office counters in 2004.

like – declaring sternly, "These have no place in a stamp album." Ironically, the Williams brothers were assiduous collectors of all things Cinderella and for many years were the joint editors of *The Cinderella Philatelist*.

BEYOND THE CATALOGUE
What is the definition of a philatelic Cinderella? The short answer is anything that is not listed in the standard stamp catalogues. However, this simple answer has to be qualified, for general stamp catalogues often omit items that do find a place in the more specialized catalogues, and quite often what the editor decides to include is arbitrary. For example, some catalogues, especially in Europe, list and price automatic machine stamps, often known as ATM (from the German term *Automatenmarken*), but sometimes referred to loosely as Framas, after the Swiss company that pioneered them. In Britain they are referred to as vending machine labels, and that last word tends to be applied to anything that is not a stamp – despite the fact that the Penny Black and other early British stamps were described in their own sheet margins as labels.

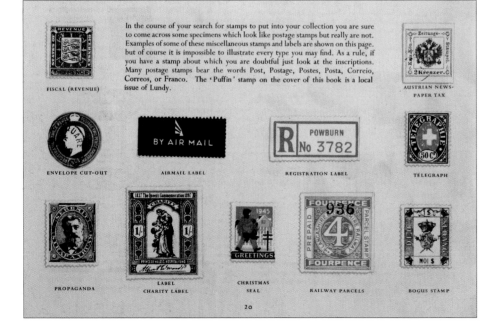

Civil War Cinderellas

These patriotic labels were created around 1861 by the Federal government during the American Civil War. They were produced in sheets (size unknown) of at least 9 images in *se-tenant* blocks. The right-hand image displays one of the labels in place, bound to the envelope by means of a town cancellation – a rare occurrence. The biblical reference shown at the top of this mounted label (Job 39:21) reads: "He paweth in the valley, and rejoiceth in his strength; he goeth on to meet the armed men." Any literate person in those days would have understood its relevance to the war.

Service Indicator Labels – The New Cinderellas?

Postage dues are not postage stamps, as they do not indicate that postage has been prepaid, and for that reason they are strictly termed labels – yet they are invariably included in stamp dealers' catalogues. The distinction between "stamps" (items included in the catalogues) and "labels" (ignored by the catalogues) is becoming more and more blurred. In recent years, for example, the UK has adopted service indicator labels, computer-printed at the point of sale, and these have now virtually ousted the higher denominations of conventional stamps. They prepay postage and perform all the functions of traditional stamps, yet they are completely ignored by the catalogues. Collectors, on the other hand, have had the good sense to realize that these things are just as worthy of study and collecting as the pretty pictures known as commemorative and special issues, most of which never perform any actual postal duty and merely serve to raise revenue for the postal services.

Many other countries operate a similar system. In the USA, in particular, such self-adhesive labels have been available at postal counters for many years. In fact, the difference between conventional stamps (more and more of which are produced to generate philatelic sales) and operational labels (which are gradually usurping the traditional role of stamps in prepaying postage) is becoming difficult to define. Catalogues continue to list, price and illustrate stamps whose status is questionable and which, in many instances, never see the country from which they purport to come, while ignoring the increasing number of "service labels" that now play a vital part in the smooth operation of the mails.

Both Scott (USA) and Gibbons (UK) list the labels involved in an experimental self-service mailing system that was tried in Washington and Kensington, Maryland, in 1989–90. Gibbons describes them simply as machine labels, whereas Scott more accurately refers to them as computer-vended postage. While Gibbons illustrates and describes them, Scott lists and prices them in some detail. These different approaches are also evident in the case of the more permanent issues in use since 1992.

Neither catalogue gives space to the parcel stamps of Belgium and the Netherlands, denominated by weight, or the range of special service labels produced by Germany, all of which cost money and indicate the service provided. The moral here is "ignore the catalogues". If you are specializing in a particular country, everything to do with the postal service deserves an equal place in your collection.

POSTAGE PAID IMPRESSIONS

Businesses, local authorities and mail order companies, which at one time used a postal frank, meter mark or bulk posting prepaid in cash denoted by a special red postmark, now make extensive use of systems such as permit mailing (in the USA) or postage-paid impressions (in most other countries). These impressions, handstruck or printed, are applied either directly to the cover, card or wrapper, or to a self-adhesive label. An increasing number of postal administrations now encourage local businesses to custom their own design, upon which they will be issued with an identification number. Thanks to their propensity for unique thematic appeal and pictorial motif, PPIs have already gained many devotees, and may indeed be Cinderellas of the future.

Above: These two triangular stamps are "phantom" issues – a popular branch of Cinderella philately. They were created by a Viennese stamp dealer, S. Friedl, to commemorate the discovery of a group of glacial islands during an Austro-Hungarian expedition attempting to reach the North Pole in 1872–4. The green item names "Cap Pest", the yellow refers to "Cap Wien". The pair is much sought after by collectors of polar issues.

SOCIAL PHILATELY

This is the newest branch of the hobby of stamp collecting, having originated in Australia in the late 1990s. In 1999 a competitive class for social philately was inaugurated at the Melbourne International Philatelic Exhibition. The concept spread to the Northern Hemisphere shortly afterwards, when it was included in the London Stamp Show of May 2000. It was basically a reaction against the strictures of the traditional and thematic philately classes in national and international competitions, which disqualified exhibitors if they strayed off the straight and narrow path laid down by the rules.

If an exhibitor included items that were not strictly stamps, either mint or affixed to covers or cards, the exhibit was severely marked down. More and more collectors were finding these restrictions increasingly irksome. They felt that – far from detracting from their displays – the judicial inclusion

Below: A page from a collection devoted to the floating mail of St Kilda.

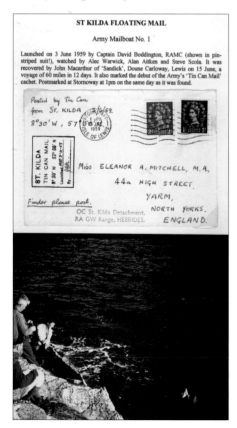

of non-philatelic items, such as ephemera or photographs, that were relevant to the stamps made the exhibit far more interesting, especially to the general public, who would not necessarily appreciate a show devoted to stamps alone. There was a very real danger of philately becoming esoteric and elitist, and the gulf between the "pot hunter" dedicated to winning competitions and the ordinary collector was becoming wider every year. More importantly, however, as competitive philately became more rarefied and confined, the potential for attracting and recruiting newcomers to the hobby decreased sharply. Competitive displays were beginning to appear boring to many collectors, let alone the general public.

A NEW WAY TO COLLECT

Recognizing this problem, the organizers of philatelic shows tentatively suggested an Open Class where anything was permissible and entries were judged by popular vote. However, this merely represented an extension of the existing system and ran the risk of becoming subject to similar rules and regulations if aspiring winners hoped to progress beyond it.

It was the collector Pat Grimwood-Taylor, exhibiting for the very first time at Melbourne in 1999, who became the apostle of a new style. She scooped a gold medal at the exhibition and subsequently conducted a seminar on the subject in London, for which the British Philatelic Trust (BPT) produced an attractive pamphlet under the title *What is SOCIAL PHILATELY?* Marking further recognition for the new concept, the definition hinged on the aim of presenting a historical story or illustrating the relevance or impact of a postal system – official or otherwise – within a society.

Straight away, the two fundamental differences between social philately and other forms of collecting were made

clear. You do not necessarily have to be an expert philatelist (though a knowledge of the basic techniques of the hobby is a help) and, more importantly, you can include many types of non-philatelic material and ephemera (such as maps, prints, coins, medals, cigarette cards and banknotes) in your collection to make it tell the story.

USING POSTAL HISTORY

The BPT leaflet went on to expand its theme, explaining that you can tell the story of the development of a town or country by using stamps, actual letters and documents of all kinds. Local postal historians have probably been doing this for many years, expanding their interests far beyond the strict boundaries of postal markings and covers or postcards.

Leaflets and mini-posters announcing changes in postal rates or the opening or closure of post offices are strictly relevant, but what about press-cuttings containing human interest stories such as postal workers being bitten by dogs or retiring after 60 years in the service? This kind of material had always previously been something of a grey area, considered suitable for a talk to a local philatelic society, but not for inclusion in a competitive display.

In studying the postal history of a town or locality, the philatelist inevitably becomes immersed in the social and economic development of the place, amassing plenty of material that is fascinating but not actually relevant to the story of the posts. Social philately allows the collector to probe the background of a historic event, or chain of events, and include both conventional and non-conventional philatelic material to tell the tale.

A PERSONAL STUDY OF ST KILDA

Relating this to my own experience, and arising out of time I spent with the British Army on the remote island of St Kilda in 1959–61, I formed a collection of that island's postal history that eventually ran to nine volumes. From the outset, however, I was not content merely to acquire covers and postally used postcards bearing the single-circle datestamp, or even explore

Below: Another page on the floating mail of St Kilda, showing a letter sent in this manner in 1897 and a photograph of an original "mailboat" complete with sheep's bladder float.

ST KILDA FLOATING MAIL
Letter to Richard Kearton from William Macdonald on 2 January 1897 but wrongly dated 1896. 'I your dear friend' on the reverse.

The Kearton mailboat of 1897
The letters were rolled up tightly and placed in a tiny medicine bottle inside the hull

by-ways such as the island's unique floating mail, airdrops, emergency helicopter flights or mail carried from St Kilda by French lobster-boats and Spanish trawlers that ended up in Camaret-sur-Mer or San Sebastian.

I added maps, ranging from that of Martin Martin, the first visitor to describe the island in detail in 1698, to a contemporary flight plan for one of the earliest airdrops in 1959. Ephemera in the collection ranged from leaflets produced by the National Trust for Scotland (who now own the island) to a spoof certificate purporting to be from King Neptune and retrieved from a bottle washed up on the shore. This was one of several thousands launched off the east coast of the USA in 1959 as a stunt celebrating the bicentenary of the Guinness brewery; most of the bottles came ashore in America but some drifted all the way across the Atlantic on the Gulf Stream. This find also gave me the opportunity to include a Guinness bicentenary beer-bottle label, arguably the first commemorative of its kind, which had been included with Neptune's parchment inside the bottle.

FLOATING MAILS

The earliest letter I possess from St Kilda dates from 1738. It has no wrapper or postmark and would probably have been disqualified in any conventional postal history display, despite its immense historical interest. It is a letter written by Lady Grange, who was kidnapped in Edinburgh by friends of her ex-husband and eventually imprisoned on St Kilda for fear that she would expose her husband's implication in a Jacobite plot. Her letter, written in ink "from the soot of my lamp and mine awin blood", was discovered three years later in a half-buried whisky bottle on the beach at Baleshare, an island of the Outer Hebrides. It eventually found its way to the addressee, her cousin in Edinburgh, but by the time he took action the poor woman had been moved to the Isle of Skye, where she

ST KILDA FLOATING MAIL
Report in the *Scottish Daily Mail* of 23 July 1959; the allusion to Arch to Arc referred to a joint-Services race from London to Paris.

Rocketmen's mail goes faster by tin can

Above: Newspaper cuttings are a useful adjunct to a social philately collection.

Right: Parchment found in a Guinness bottle launched in the 1950s.

died. This letter, and the covering note from the tenant of Baleshare, form the basis of my own social philately display of the floating mails of St Kilda, developed by the islands in the 1870s and continuing until 1930 when the island was evacuated.

Reoccupied by the RAF and the Army in 1957, and regularly visited since by work parties from the National Trust for Scotland, St Kilda has been the scene of many "mailboat" or "tin can mail" launches over the past 45 years. Some have been picked up on the west coast of the Hebrides within 48 hours, while others were recovered more than three years later, as far away as eastern Iceland and north Norway, Orkney and Shetland.

Although the collection includes stamps, postmarks, cachets, charge marks, mixed franking of British and Norwegian stamps and even postage due labels (on covers recovered abroad and treated as unpaid because British stamps are not valid in Norway), the bulk of the display is devoted to photographs of launches and recoveries and a mass of press cuttings and articles about this remarkable phenomenon. It is entirely two-dimensional because I have not yet acquired one of the actual mailboats, consisting of a piece of driftwood hollowed out to form the hull, attached to an inflated sheep's bladder.

FORGERIES, FANTASIES AND POSTAL FRAUD

The subject of stamp forgery attracts collectors, not simply because of the tales of derring-do often attached, but also due to the challenge presented by comparing the likeness between real and fake. Forgery has dogged stamp-issuing authorities since the birth of the Penny Black. British authorities hired an American inventor, Jacob Perkins, who devised a rose engine capable of producing such an intricate background that the forger would be deterred. In fact, only one attempt to forge the Penny Black was detected, and that was such a poor travesty that it was easily spotted.

VICTIMS OF STAMP FORGERY

Countries where cheaper processes such as letterpress and lithography were in use, or where postal authorities paid

Above: In a bid to beat the forgers, the Twopence Blue was issued with check letters in all four corners in July 1858. The combination of numbers identified each stamp's position in a printed sheet.

Below: These British 6d stamps were produced in doubly fugitive ink with the value surcharged in red letters – another attempt to deter fraudulent use.

less attention to good intaglio engraving, often fell victim to forgery. The earliest attempts at forgery were usually intended to defraud the revenue.

Yet even the British postal service was not exempt from this humiliation. The 1s stamp was forged in 1872–3 and vast quantities were passed off as genuine at the Stock Exchange (where this denomination was commonly used on telegrams), but the crime did not come to light until 1898, by which time the trail had gone cold. It was thanks to the vigilance of philatelists that the forgery was detected at all, because the counterfeiters had used combinations of corner letters that did not exist in the genuine stamps. Although the Post Office placed its faith in the check letters as a deterrent to forgery, postal staff apparently never gave them a second glance. Today, the Stock Exchange forgeries fetch higher prices at auction than the genuine stamps, such is the demand for them.

Postal forgeries continue to this day. In recent years British and French definitives have been forged for sale to the public at discount prices, and it was for this reason that elliptical perforations were introduced, the theory being that forgers might produce a passable imitation of a stamp but they would never get the perforations right.

FAMOUS FORGERS

Once philately became an established hobby and definite market values emerged for the scarcer stamps, it was inevitable that the stamp trade should be infiltrated by unscrupulous people who turned to forgery as a means of robbing gullible collectors. The activities of such master forgers as François Fournier, Erasmus Oneglia, Jean de Sperati, S. Allan Taylor and Albert C. Roessler are well documented in literature such as Varro E. Tyler's *Philatelic Forgers: Their Lives and Works* (1976) and, indeed, some important collections of their wares have been formed.

Many forgers achieved notoriety in their day. S. Allan Taylor, an American born in Ayrshire, Scotland, in 1838, was known as "the Prince of Forgers" and produced hundreds of fakes and forgeries during the latter half of the 19th century, some of which were assumed to be authentic for many decades. He put his own portrait on bogus charity and local post stamps, and a self-likeness of the mature Taylor was incorporated into a label produced by a short-lived group of admiring Cinderella philatelists, the S. Allan Taylor Society.

An accomplished forger of more recent times, the Italian Jean de Sperati (1884–1957) was the most technically competent of his peers, producing some 566 forgeries purporting to originate from more than 100 countries.

Bogus Bill

Abkhazia, which seceded from Georgia, briefly had a genuine postal service with distinctive stamps, but long after the secession was suppressed stamps continued to appear in its name, including a notorious miniature sheet showing President Clinton and Monica Lewinsky. Georgia even apologized to the Clinton family and offered them a free holiday at the Black Sea resort of Soukhumi in recompense.

Above: Genuine and forged versions of the French 25c Hermes, the latter produced by British Intelligence.

He even wrote books on the art of philatelic forgery, in which he expressed his contempt for the "experts" who had tried to foil his efforts.

COLLECTING FORGERIES

Many of these colourful characters had a taste for risk and illegality, and no doubt relished the thrill of creating immaculate forgeries that fooled even the most diligent of postal watchdogs. But there are other instances of forgery,

Below: Bogus stamps attributed to South Moluccas, New Atlantis, Albania, Atlantis and Sedang.

A Dishonest Postmaster

Fraudulent usage of postal material does not always involve the forgery or manipulation of stamps. This rare envelope, shown here front and back, which eventually arrived at Everest Base Camp in 1936, informs the recipient that their letter "Suffered detention in Gangtok post office owing to the Postmaster's failure to affix postage stamps and to forward them in time. The Postmaster has been sent to jail for his offence."

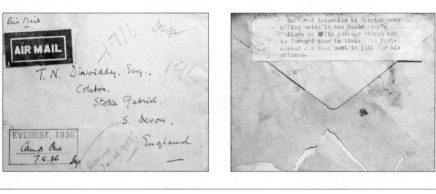

where the primary motive – financial gain – appears to lack a well thought out plan. Where stamps are plentiful and cheap in the genuine state, it does not seem to have been worth the forger's expertise to perpetrate such imitations. Nevertheless this is not as unusual a phenomenon as might be thought. Many stamp clubs have a forgery collection, which members may consult in order to check doubtful specimens in their own collections.

Many of the forgeries produced in the 19th century would fool no one nowadays, either because the wrong printing process was used (such as lithography instead of intaglio) or because the draughtsmanship was relatively crude, but it must be remembered that 19th-century collectors did not have the well-illustrated reference works so readily available nowadays. The study of forgeries is germane to any specialized collection, which explains why forgeries often fetch high prices at auction, even when clearly exposed for what they are.

PROPAGANDA FORGERIES

Arguably the most desirable of all forgeries are those that were manufactured by various belligerents in wartime as part of a propaganda campaign. During World War I, Britain forged German and Bavarian stamps, which were affixed to letters or cards dropped in enemy or neutral countries to give the impression of coming from Germany while disseminating subtle propaganda or defeatist literature. This worked well enough to encourage the British to repeat the exercise in World War II, but this time they produced clever parodies of Nazi stamps as well. Stamps of the Vichy French regime portraying Marshal Petain were also forged by the British.

The Germans were adept at creating propaganda forgeries of British stamps, including a large number of George VI definitives overprinted "Liquidation of Empire" and the parody of the 1937 Coronation stamp, with Stalin replacing Queen Elizabeth.

BOGUS STAMPS

The term "bogus" describes stamps that are pure fantasies, often purporting to come from non-existent countries. This was a favourite ploy of conmen in the late 19th century, using such stamps to lure investors in fictional colonial projects. Sadly, these fabrications have their modern counterparts. The break-up of the Soviet Union in the 1990s proved to be a fertile ground for a host of bogus issues, aimed at unsuspecting philatelic buyers.

FIRST DAY COVERS AND SPECIAL POSTMARKS

In the 1930s, when postal administrations began announcing impending issues of stamps (instead of just putting them on sale without warning), collectors got into the habit of mailing covers to themselves with the latest stamps purchased on the day they became available. Before that decade was out many countries were cashing in on the growing popularity of this trend by providing special postmarks for use on the first day of issue.

FIRST DAY COVERS

Both stationers and stamp dealers published attractive envelopes to accompany the new issues, and by the 1940s many postal services were getting in on this act as well. By 1950 the collecting of first day covers – or FDCs as they are known for short – was well established, although it was not until 1963 that the British Post Office began to produce first day postmarks and souvenir envelopes.

This field has now developed to such an extent that most collectors acquire both a mint set and the appropriate FDC for each new issue. In addition to the special handstamp or machine cancellation authorized by the postal service for each issue, many dealers, cover producers and organizations (such as the charity or public body connected with a particular stamp issue) sponsor first day handstamps. In Britain, for example, as many as 40 sponsored postmarks may be associated with each new issue.

SPECIAL POSTMARKS

Though the use of operational datestamps on ordinary mail has declined, the fashion for special handstamps remains undiminished. These originated in the mid-19th century, when temporary post offices were set up at major agricultural fairs and exhibitions and gradu-

ally extended to all manner of events, from conferences to sports and race meetings. At these post offices a specially worded postmark was invariably applied, but since the 1960s it has become more usual merely to have a posting box at such events, the mail being cancelled at the nearest main post office. Many countries use pictorial postmarks as a form of local publicity and they exist both as handstamps and as machine cancellations. Postal administrations sometimes offer special

Right: First day covers from Gibraltar and the Czech Republic – on the latter both the pictorial panel and the postmark complement the stamp.

Below: The cartoon character Phil Stamp finds a humorous angle on British stamps issued in 2004.

FDC

Above: An Indian stamp from 2004 whose motif is matched on the first day postmark.

postmarks automatically to customers who set up standing orders, but in other countries the collector still has to write to the individual post office and send items for reposting.

THE PHILATELIC DOCUMENT

France pioneered the philatelic document in 1973, originally as a means of raising funds for its National Postal Museum. The document consists of a sheet describing a particular issue, with a stamp affixed and cancelled by a special postmark. The concept has spread to the USA and many other countries in recent years. Pre-stamped envelopes and postcards are also often produced in connection with stamp exhibitions and are avidly collected with the appropriate stamps and cancellations.

CHOOSING BETWEEN POSTMARK AND PICTURE

Around the beginning of the 20th century, when picture postcard mania was at its height, collectors attempted to match the picture on the card with a postmark relevant to it. However, there was something rather disappointing about mounting the souvenirs of your

Below: A French philatelic document bearing the Gaston Lagaffe cartoon stamp, with pictorial postmark and background text.

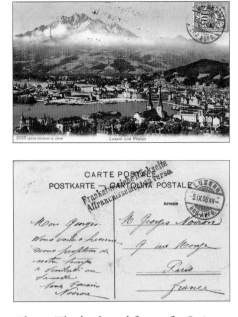

Above: The back and front of a Swiss postcard that has the stamp on the picture side.

foreign vacation in an album but being unable to see the stamp and postmark as well as the picture. This problem was solved by sticking the stamp in the top right-hand corner of the picture side and hoping that the post office would indulge your eccentric behaviour by applying the postmark.

In Britain this informal practice was officially banned until the 1970s, but other countries were more obliging and France and Germany even had special explanatory marks, struck on the address side, to explain that the adhesives were on the picture side, thus avoiding the surcharging of the card as if it had been sent unpaid.

MAXIMUM CARDS

In the 1930s, when stamps had become much more pictorial in concept, the notion arose of affixing a stamp to a postcard with a relevant picture and then getting the stamp cancelled at an appropriate place. Indeed, many postal administrations and philatelic bureaux encouraged this by producing special cards to accompany each new issue of stamps, and providing a service for cancelling them on the picture side. Such

cards are known as maximum cards because they offer the maximum of a picture, a stamp and a postmark that can all be seen at a glance when mounted in an album. While these items are important adjuncts to thematic collecting, they are now studied and collected in their own right under the name of maximaphily.

Although the British Post Office began to permit maximum cards only in 1970 (in connection with the Philympia stamp exhibition held that year), it took the idea a step further in 1973, when it introduced postcards that reproduced commemorative or special issue stamps. These are known as PHQ cards (from the initials of Postal Headquarters), and are collected either in unused condition or with the appropriate adhesive and matching first day cancellation on the picture side. Ironically, PHQ cards were very slow to catch on with collectors, and this limited circulation means that some examples now change hands for three-figure sums.

Left and below: Maximum cards from the Faroes and Australian Antarctic.

Below: British PHQ card for the English first class definitive.

POSTER STAMPS

The term "poster stamps" was devised in the interwar period, when multi-colour lithography was frequently used to create posters in miniature for the promotion of tourism. The description of such items as "stamps" is in fact a misnomer, because although they resemble stamps in appearance these bright, colourful and attractive labels have no connection with the postal services. They were produced by tourist boards, chambers of commerce and even private individuals. They were also extensively

Right: A poster stamp produced for the Leipzig Fairs of 1906–7.

Above: Something of a philatelic first, the Shakespeare Penny Memorial label both commemorated the Bard's birth and sought to fund a new theatre.

Below: A label publicizing the Pan-American Exposition in 1901.

employed to advertise the products of many companies, especially after the concept of brand names and trademarks developed in importance in the late 19th century.

COMMEMORATIVE LABELS

Although commemorative postage stamps did not materialize until the late 1880s, labels that celebrated historic personalities or documented important events were in existence many years earlier. The first of these was an embossed medallic label produced for an exhibition in Vienna; although it bore the effigy of the Emperor Ferdinand it was a private production by Apollo Kerzen-Fabrik. In 1851 a label was issued in connection with the Great Exhibition in London; in fact, there is a theory that it was devised to frank the correspondence of Royal Commissioners, but it is of such great rarity that little is known about it.

All of the early labels were produced in connection with international fairs and exhibitions, but in 1860 a label portraying Garibaldi celebrated his expedition to Sicily as part of the campaign for the unification of Italy. Garibaldi was also the subject of a label in 1863 mourning his defeat at Aspromonte. The first label to mark a historic anniversary was produced in England in 1864. Inscribed with the legend "Shakespeare Penny Memorial", it portrayed the Bard himself and celebrated the 300th anniversary of his birth. As the inscription implies, it was also intended as a fundraiser for the projected Memorial Theatre at Shakespeare's birthplace, Stratford-upon-Avon, completed in 1879.

Up to 1873 very few labels were recorded each year, but when Vienna hosted the International Exhibition that year there were embossed scalloped

Below: A French patriotic label of 1915 recalling the Revolution (left) and a German patriotic label of the same year captioned "God punish England!"

labels for the various commissioners, as well as the label reproducing the gold medals awarded, with the effigy of the Emperor Franz Joseph on the obverse.

A NEW CENTURY

The generation of commemorative labels reached its zenith at the Exposition Universelle in Paris in 1900. This exhibition, to celebrate the achievements of the previous century and progress in the next, was the greatest of the world's fairs at that time, and resulted in the issuing of many hundreds of different labels.

By the end of the 19th century, production of commemorative labels had grown enormously, with publishers producing sets of colourful labels for every conceivable occasion. The labels for the Paris show could be divided into general publicity, the numerous series that featured the landmarks and scenery of Paris, the issues of the many French learned societies, the labels published by companies advertising goods displayed at the fair and the *timbres recompensés*, reproducing the various gold, silver and bronze medals. In addition, A. Baguet alone produced five sets of labels, 40 in all, honouring each of the national pavilions. Some students of poster stamps have devoted a lifetime solely to collecting the different labels from the Exposition Universelle.

The first phase of poster stamps ended with the onset of World War I but over the next four years the publicity labels of the earlier years gave way to long sets showing regimental flags, portraits of military and naval heroes and all the weird and wonderful weaponry conjured up by the conflict. Inevitably France and Germany vied with each other in the production of labels, which moved effortlessly from publicity to propaganda.

TOURIST PUBLICITY

The return to peace saw a dramatic change in the labels. By the 1920s the notion of commemorative postage stamps was well established, and consequently far fewer labels of a commemorative nature were produced. It was now that the publicity element came into its own with the rise of cheap foreign travel. Tourist organizations were quick to perceive the benefits of advertising through this medium. Many of the rather garish posters of the period were automatically reduced to the medium of poster stamps and adorned envelopes containing promotional leaflets and brochures. There was an attempt in continental Europe to produce booklets of different scenic labels, but this fashion was already waning when the outbreak of World War II killed it off.

PHILATELIC EXHIBITIONS

One sphere in which the poster stamp has held its own, despite the vagaries of fashion or the competition from postage stamps, is in philately itself. The first issue in this connection consisted of a series of 1pf stamps of the Circular Post of Frankfurt-am-Main in 1887, available in five different colours. Since this time,

Right: A Swiss tourist label publicizing autumn holidays.

Below: A sheetlet depicting views of the Smithsonian Institution in Washington, DC.

Above: Prewar poster stamps from Tournoël in France and Newquay in Cornwall, England.

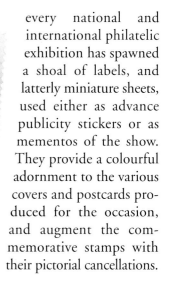

every national and international philatelic exhibition has spawned a shoal of labels, and latterly miniature sheets, used either as advance publicity stickers or as mementos of the show. They provide a colourful adornment to the various covers and postcards produced for the occasion, and augment the commemorative stamps with their pictorial cancellations.

SOCIETIES

The collecting of poster stamps is closely affiliated to Cinderella philately, and you may get information on significant issues from the societies devoted to that field. There are, however, organizations and exhibitions devoted predominantly to the study and collection of poster stamps. The American Poster Stamp Society offers membership and a regular bulletin. An address for the society can be found at the end of this book.

CHARITY SEALS AND LABELS

From the Shakespeare Penny Memorial label of 1864, an increasing number of labels were devised to raise money for good causes. Although many are not official postage stamps, and may not be listed in catalogues, their often colourful and highly visual designs make them of natural interest to collectors.

Left: The Prince of Wales's Hospital Fund label, 1897.

Below: World War I charity fundraising labels from New Zealand and Russia.

Right: Einar Holboell, who devised charity seals, was portrayed on a Belgian anti-TB stamp in 1955.

THE QUEEN'S COMMEMORATION

Queen Victoria's diamond jubilee of 1897 yielded several sets of purely commemorative labels, but there was a particular issue that stood out on account of its intricate design.

Line-engraved by De La Rue (who produced the British postage stamps) the issue consisted of 1s and 2s 6d labels, each depicting the allegorical figure of Charity aiding poor children. At the top was the inscription "1837 The Queen's Commemoration 1897" but at the foot was the facsimile signature of the Prince of Wales (the future

Edward VII) and the words "Prince of Wales's Hospital Fund". Although these labels had no postal validity they had the tacit support of the Post Office and were intended to adorn letters and postcards – so long as they were kept well away from the proper postage stamps. Used examples are scarce, suggesting that most were purchased to keep as souvenirs of the jubilee.

The success of the venture induced the promoters to issue 5s and 10s labels as well, but this was going too far and not surprisingly the high values are of the greatest rarity today. The resultant fiasco put a damper on attempts to repeat the exercise and it is significant that no fundraising labels appeared in Britain at the time of the Boer War (1899–1902). There was a belated resurgence during World War I though the idea found greater favour in India and Australia than it did in Britain. Nevertheless, charity labels are among the most enduring of the Cinderellas on a worldwide basis, despite the fierce competition from charity stamps.

CHRISTMAS AND EASTER SEALS

It was in December 1904 that a Danish postal official, Einar Holboell, came up with the notion of producing labels to

be affixed to the envelopes of greetings cards, the money thus raised being given to the national anti-tuberculosis fund. His idea was enthusiastically endorsed by the Danish Post Office, which even arranged for the Christmas seals to be sold at post offices. The scheme was taken up by the other Scandinavian countries the following year. At first a single design was produced annually, but in more recent years different motifs have appeared on each label, often forming a composite design covering the sheet. Holboell has himself been portrayed on charity stamps of Denmark and Belgium.

The labels spread to the Faroes, Iceland, Greenland and the Danish West Indies (now the American Virgin Islands), and from there spread to

Above: A booklet containing French anti-TB Christmas seals.

Below: This Swedish envelope bears the 1903 Christmas seal alongside a stamp.

Korean Charity Labels
It is easy to detect the American influence on these labels for Boys Town and Girls Town charities in Korea, which by the 1960s were caring for almost 4,000 orphans in the cities of Pusan and Seoul.

Above: Even charity seals occasionally carried commercial advertising. This French booklet pane promotes various items, such as toothpaste, in its margins.

many other countries, notably Canada, Mexico, the USA, France and South Africa. In the last two countries the seals were produced in booklets, which

Below: A bilingual pair of Christmas seals from South Africa (1938).

Above: A Danish Christmas seal (1904) and a Thorvaldsen Foundation seal from Iceland (1953).

Below: An Easter seal produced by the St John Ambulance Brigade, 1970.

were sold at post offices. French stamp booklets carried commercial advertising on the top and bottom margins, and this practice was extended to the charity labels, often with incongruous results. A factor unifying most Christmas seals, no matter where they are issued, is the red Cross of Lorraine, the international emblem of the anti-tuberculosis campaign.

In the 1940s the concept was extended to Easter seals, which were sold in aid of funds for the handicapped. Recurring themes of these labels were the Easter lily or a crutch to symbolize the disabled. In New Zealand, however, Easter seals support the St John Ambulance movement and incorporate the Maltese Cross emblem. In recent years many other charities have begun producing their own versions of Christmas and Easter seals to raise funds for cancer research, epilepsy and the prevention of blindness, while organizations like the Red Cross issue charity labels in many lands that can be used all year round.

CHILDREN'S CHARITIES

A group of charity labels with a strong thematic appeal is that devoted to the care of orphans and homeless children. The vast majority of Easter seals come into this category, notably the American labels showing disabled children overcoming their handicap, accompanied by slogans such as "I'm a fighter" or "Back a fighter".

The best known of the children's charities producing annual labels is Boys Town in Nebraska, founded by Father Edward Flanagan. Many of its

Above: Christmas seals from Boys Town, Nebraska and Cal Farley's Boys Ranch, Texas.

Left: Dürer's "Praying Hands" on a Christmas seal of the Omaha Home for Boys.

labels feature the poignant figure of a boy with a youngster asleep round his neck, saying, "He ain't heavy, Father, He's m' brother." Based on a real incident that has since been immortalized in a statue, this motif is the logo of Boys Town. Separate labels exist for affiliated Boys' and Children's home charities.

Below: Charity labels issued by France and Spain. The French Red Cross label (left) raised funds for military hospitals during World War I; the Spanish "2 pesetas" was one of a number produced in the 1930s and '40s to help provide for the widows of postal workers.

FISCAL STAMPS AND SPECIAL SERVICE LABELS

Adhesive stamps and labels issued to denote dutiable goods, payment of a licence, or simply bearing special instructions to customs or to postal authorities, are among the most diverse of Cinderella collectables.

FISCAL STAMPS

Adhesive stamps embossed on deep blue "sugar-bag" paper were used for revenue purposes at the Board of Stamps and Taxes in London from 1694 onwards. They were an innovation imported by William of Orange from his native Holland, where they had been in use since the early 17th century. Later fiscal stamps (known as revenue stamps in the United States) were embossed directly on to boxes and bottles containing patent medicines, or the wrappers of dice, while the elaborate device on the ace of spades in a deck of cards was, in fact, a tax stamp.

The excise duty on a wide range of articles, from hair powder to gloves, was indicated by such stamps. Adhesive stamps were produced in perforated sheets for matchboxes, tobacco and

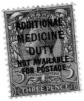

Left: A British 3d postage stamp over-printed for use as an additional medicine duty stamp.

Above: A patent medicine tax stamp, used to seal pill boxes.

Below: Fiscal stamps of the Cape of Good Hope and Malta.

cigarettes, wines and spirits, entertainment duty and even phonograph records. The range of fiscal stamps in Britain in the 19th and early 20th centuries was enormous, from additional medicine duty during World War I to travel permits and unemployment insurance. As a result of the Local Stamp Act of 1869 there were even revenue stamps of purely local validity, from Alderney to Winchester, and separate issues for Scotland and Ireland. Savings stamps, introduced in many countries in World War I, continued until the 1970s and have since been replaced by individual issues by banks and public utilities.

A similar pattern operated in many other countries, with a wide range of national duties and numerous taxes

Below: A US cigarette tax stamp portraying De Witt Clinton, a documentary stamp featuring a battleship, and an Ohio vendor's receipt stamp.

Below: The US migratory bird hunting stamp for 1954: the design was changed annually to feature different species.

imposed at cantonal or communal level. In the USA it was illegal to use a revenue stamp for any purpose other than the specific tax inscribed on it, and up to 1862 there was a proliferation of stamps for many duties. Thereafter a general issue of documentary stamps by the Bureau of Internal Revenue could be used indiscriminately with the exception of the distinctive stamps applied to proprietory articles, such as matches and medicines, introduced in 1871. In 1962 the centenary of the documentary stamps was marked by what is probably the world's first commemorative revenue stamp, and facilities were exceptionally made for it to be used on first day covers. The use of such stamps ceased in 1967.

In 1934 the USA introduced migratory bird hunting permits and stamps denoting payment of the fee. In addition, many individual states have their own annual migratory hunting stamps.

TELEGRAPH, TELEPHONE AND TELEVISION STAMPS

At one time there were separate issues of stamps for telegrams in many countries, as well as the issues of the private

Above: Telegraph stamps issued by Britain, Spain and Tangier.

Left: A British telephone stamp of 1884.

telegraph companies. In Britain, the National Telephone Company even had its own stamps (1884–91) portraying its chairman, Colonel Robert Raynsford-Jackson. They were used as an early method to pay for telephone calls at local offices, to avoid the need for an exchange of money. The stamps were finally withdrawn from use in 1891, due to the Post Office's belief that they could be confused with normal postage stamps. Despite this, special stamps were used until relatively recently in some countries to help people save towards the cost of a TV licence.

POSTAL SERVICE LABELS

Labels denoting specific postal services originated in the 1870s when Germany and Sweden introduced stickers bearing names of towns and serial numbers for use on registered packets. The system was later extended to the serial labels affixed to the cards that accompanied parcels. In Britain, distinctive parcel labels were issued to every post office from 1883 to 1916, but registration labels were not adopted until 1907, although the UPU had decreed this in 1881. Distinctive serial labels have also been used for certified mail (USA) or recorded delivery (UK), with

equivalents in most other countries. In recent years labels distinctive to each post office have been largely replaced by a national series of barcode labels. Resealing labels for damaged or broken packets and explanatory labels marked "Deceased", "Gone away" and "Return to sender" in different languages are also to be found.

AIRMAIL *ETIQUETTES*

France pioneered special stickers for airmail in 1918, and for that reason they are still generally known to collectors by the French term *etiquettes*. Their use is on the increase as it is now mandatory to affix them to all letters and cards going abroad by air. In many countries nowadays their place has been taken by A-Priority labels, although these retain the general pattern of white inscriptions on a blue background. In such countries there is usually the equivalent of a second-class service denoted by white on green B-Economy labels. The Postal

Above: Reasons for non-delivery are explained in English, Afrikaans and French on this South African label.

Below: A pre-stamped postcard from the Åland Islands, bearing an airmail "priority" sticker, issued in 2004.

Union Congress at Madrid in 1920 decreed the introduction of green labels for Customs declaration and these, in various modifications, are still in use, generally inscribed in French and a national language. For dutiable goods on which the tax has been paid there are labels inscribed in French "*Franc de droits*"(Free of dues).

LABELS FOR SPECIAL TREATMENT

At various times from the late 19th century there have been special labels for express and special delivery services, warning labels affixed to parcels of eggs or containing fragile or perishable substances, and even labels for packages containing live creatures, pathological specimens or radioactive materials. There are also stickers to mark parcels containing Braille reading material for the blind. These labels often conform to an international convention of easily recognizable symbols, such as a wine glass (fragile), a rabbit (live animals), the staff of Aesculapius (pathological specimens) or a blind person carrying a white stick.

Right: A label from the Czech Republic for use on parcels containing live animals.

Right: An early United States Customs label.

Below: An insured parcel card for a dispatch from Vienna to Berne in 1911, bearing an impressed 10 heller stamp.

LOCAL STAMPS AND PRIVATE POSTS

The stamp catalogues of the 19th century included postage stamps of all kinds, whether issued by government posts or local services operated by private enterprise. Later, the sheer number of government issues forced all but a few highly specialized one-country catalogues to drop nearly everything else. Thus the stamps of the many local and private posts were consigned to limbo.

Above: Two stamps used for the Chesterfield Scouts Christmas post.

Left: Shotts Scouts in Lanarkshire, Scotland, produced this 75th anniversary stamp for their 1998 Christmas postal service.

CARRIERS' STAMPS

US carrier stamps are among the few semi-official issues that continue to be listed. These local stamps originate from the period before 1863, the year the US Post Office finally established a general town delivery. For some 20 to 30 years prior to this, the gap was filled by numerous local dispatch posts known as "carriers", many employees of which later worked for the government as part of the national postal network. In 1842, a 3c carrier stamp became the first ever stamp to be issued under government authority, thanks to the merging of a private firm, City Despatch Post, and the state-run New York City Carrier Department. US carrier stamps are comprehensively listed in the Scott *Specialized Catalogue of U.S. Stamps*, but ignored everywhere else.

Left and below: Two undenominated stamps, depicting Benjamin Franklin and the American eagle, produced in 1861–3 to denote the 1c charged for delivering mail from US post offices to householders. Their use was confined to New York, Philadelphia and New Orleans.

In Germany, from the 1860s to 1900, the Reichspost did not provide a service for commercial mail and printed matter such as circulars, and it was left to private operators to fill the gap. Over 200 services came into existence, many functioning within a single town and others maintaining a nationwide network. In March 1900 they were nationalized and absorbed into the Reichspost. Their heyday was the 1880s and 1890s and they pioneered various issues such as commemoratives, mourning stamps and Christmas or New Year greetings stamps. Similar local services, complete with distinctive adhesives and pre-stamped stationery, operated in Denmark, Norway and Sweden during the same period.

ZEMSTVO POSTS

By far the largest network of local posts was that operating in tsarist Russia. The imperial post served only the cities and larger towns, and in 1864 local authorities were empowered to establish their own postal services in rural districts and to link them to the imperial service. The stamps issued by these local posts are popularly known as "zemstvos" (from the Russian word for a unit of local government). Vetlonga established its service in 1865 but the honour of issuing the first stamps went to Schluesselburg the following year. From 1870 onwards the zemstvo posts were given a completely free hand in matters of design and some of the most colourful stamps of the 19th century resulted.

By the time these services were closed down as a result of the 1917 uprising by the Bolsheviks, many

Right: A Russian zemstvo stamp from Lebedyansk, showing the civic emblem, a swan.

The World's Rarest Stamp

There are quite a few stamps of which only a solitary example has been recorded, but this zemstvo stamp, issued in June 1869 by Kotelnich, in the Viatka province north-east of Moscow, is truly unique, since only half the stamp is now known to exist. It consisted of a right-hand square that was affixed to the letter while the left-hand portion was intended to be retained by the sender as a receipt. Strangely, the complete stamp was illustrated in the catalogue published in the 1880s by the Belgian dealer, Jean-Baptiste Moens.

Above: Two local ¹/₂d stamps dating from 1865–7, issued by Clark & Co of Edinburgh and the Circular Delivery Company in Glasgow.

thousands of different stamps had been released. They include the world's rarest stamp, that from Kotelnich (illustrated in the box opposite).

CIRCULAR DELIVERY STAMPS

In 1865 a number of circular delivery companies, set up to carry mail to designated households and districts, sprang up in Britain, undercutting the postal service with rates of ¹/₂d or ¹/₄d for the delivery of printed matter. In a court case of 1867 they were held to infringe the Postmaster General's monopoly and suppressed, but the Post Office was eventually obliged to lower postal rates in 1870 and allow printed matter – including newspapers and companies' advertising postcards – to be sent by post for ¹/₂d.

OTHER LOCAL POSTS

Although the heyday of the local posts was the late 19th century, there have been some interesting developments in more recent years. In 1929 M.C.

Below: One of a series of stamps issued by the Suez Canal Company in 1868 for mail conveyed by its ships.

Harman, the proprietor of Lundy Island in the Bristol Channel (who also held the mail contract), began issuing his own stamps to defray the costs of transmission of mail to and from Bideford, the nearest mainland post office. To the present day, close to 400 different stamps have been produced and the Lundy issues have a worldwide following. In the 1960s, however, several islands off the Scottish coast also began issuing stamps ostensibly to pay for local carriage, but in fact to a large extent promoted by dealers in popular themes such as Kennedy, Churchill and space travel – subjects that were irrelevant to the islands themselves. To be sure, the issues that have stayed the course have maintained their integrity and cater to real needs.

Since 1981 the Royal Mail's monopoly has been waived by the British Telecommunications Act to allow church and youth groups to organize local posts between 25 November and 1 January. Mail is collected and delivered by volunteers and the modest fee for greetings cards handled by these posts goes to charity. Most of the services produce stamps and these have become very popular with collectors.

TRANSPORTATION COMPANIES AND AIRLINES

Postal services have been run by many shipping lines and freight companies, especially in underdeveloped parts of the world where government services were either sporadic or non-existent. Many private railway companies have enjoyed the privilege of transporting mail, and stamps for this purpose – often categorized with fiscal stamps – have been employed in countries as far apart as Denmark and Australia. The conveyance of parcels has often fallen to local carriers who produced distinctive stamps for this purpose. Similarly, commercial airlines in many countries issued stamps to cover the fees charged on letters and parcels carried over their routes. Several remote islands around Britain have a private service conveying their mail to the nearest post office

and for this purpose local carriage labels are often employed. Where a regional dialect is spoken, these local stamps may have bilingual inscriptions.

POSTAL DEREGULATION

In the course of the 20th century most of the private or semi-official services were suppressed or taken over by the government posts, but from the 1980s onwards this trend has been gradually reversed. Postal services have now been deregulated in many countries. In Britain, for example, courier companies are now permitted to carry letter mail so long as they charge at least 50p for the service, and a similar proviso exists in Germany. Elsewhere, notably in Holland and Sweden, private local posts have proliferated in recent years. In New Zealand, the service known as Pete's Post and other private companies provide a feeder service for New Zealand Post, and conversely mail bearing their stamps is often delivered by the government posts.

An interesting development in the past decade has been contract remailing, whereby mail from country A is air-freighted to country B and then sorted and forwarded to country C. Apart from the extraordinary permutations this produces, it has also given rise to the issue of private stamps by carriers such as TNT, which are affixed to tourist postcards everywhere from Spain and Italy to Australia, then flown to European hubs for sorting and transmission. The stamps associated with these services are often referred to in inscriptions as "Post paid tickets".

Below: This local stamp produced by the Scottish Isle of Canna is inscribed in both English and Gaelic.

ESSAYS, ARTWORK AND PROOFS

Postage stamps do not materialize out of thin air. In most cases a considerable amount of planning is involved and many months may elapse between the commissioning of an artist to produce a suitable design and the release of the finished product to post offices and other retail outlets.

Each stage in the evolution of a stamp yields a certain amount of material, all of which is of immense interest to the truly dedicated specialist. Much of it is rare, if not unique, and inevitably it usually commands very high prices, so you have to be not only very committed to your hobby but also wealthy enough to afford it. In the end, however, it is this material that makes the difference between a good collection and one that stands a chance of winning a gold medal in competitive philatelic exhibitions.

ESSAYS AND ORIGINAL ARTWORK

An essay is a design that has been submitted for a forthcoming stamp but is rejected. Strangely, such "unadopted designs", as they are also known, often seem superior to the design that is eventually selected. Either way, essays are of interest as examples of what might have been.

In many cases, even when designs are accepted they are subject to modification and it is therefore possible to find a whole series of stages of a design, progressing from the artist's original concept through minor alterations to the finished model.

Original artwork came to prominence in the 1960s, when stamps were produced by one or other of the processes that involved photographing the artist's drawing or watercolour. In addition to these miniature works of art, with or without the overlays for lettering, value and standard features (such as the monarch's head or a coat of arms), the preliminary pen and ink thumbnail sketches are fascinating as they show how the design gradually evolved in the artist's mind.

DIE AND PLATE PROOFS

In the days when the vast majority of stamps were produced by intaglio (line-engraving or recess-printing) or typography (letterpress or relief-printing), the artist's drawing would be passed to an engraver who sat down at his bench and worked with burins and other tools to produce a master die. In intaglio, the engraver cut the design into a piece of soft steel, which was then chemically hardened. A soft steel cylinder was rolled over it under great pressure, transferring the design to the cylinder. In turn it was hardened then

Above: Die proofs of the engraved portraits used for a pair of Swedish stamps issued in 2004.

rolled the required number of times over a sheet of soft steel to produce the printing plate.

In relief-printing the engraver might work in soft metal or even a block of wood. A plaster mould would be taken from this and lead "clichés" produced. A thin layer of copper might be deposited by electrolysis and the clichés locked together in a "forme" to make the printing plate.

At each stage the master die, intermediate punches, secondary dies (with different denominations engraved on them), transfer roller and finished plate might be checked by inking them and taking a proof on soft card, India paper or some other material. These die and plate proofs might be endorsed "Before hardening" or "After hardening" and annotated with the date and the initials of the printer or examiner.

Die proofs usually appear as single impressions in pieces of card or paper with wide margins all round, whereas

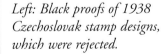

Left: Black proofs of 1938 Czechoslovak stamp designs, which were rejected.

Right: This photograph of a flat-bed cylinder press is an early example of intaglio printing. The press itself can still be seen at Somerset House in London.

Lewis and Clark Commemorative Issue

On 27 April 1954, the US Post Office announced a new 3c stamp to mark the the anniversary of the Lewis and Clark Expedition to Sioux City, Iowa. Six designs were submitted by Charles R. Chickering of the PO Bureau of Printing and Engraving – the one finally approved appears top left. Chickering's figures were inspired by the Lewis and Clark Monument at Charlottesville, Virginia, and the statue of Sacagawea – the Indian woman who guided the explorers and helped them gain the friendship of the Shoshone Indians – at the State Capitol grounds, North Dakota.

stamps without perforations may also be encountered with some form of overprint, either "Cancelled" or "Specimen" or the equivalent in another language. These items were often circulated among postal officials but were overprinted to prevent anyone trying to use them on mail.

ADDING COLOURS

With the advent of multicolour printing it became customary to take proofs of each colour separation, both individually, and in the combinations that culminated in a complete design. These are known as progressive proofs. Proofs in unadopted colours or those finally selected for the finished stamps were sometimes overprinted or punched to provide the printer with samples that could be shown to prospective clients from other postal administrations. Sometimes printers would opt to use imperforate stamps for this purpose, overprinted of course to prevent them being used postally.

Nowadays presentation packs are available from post offices along with mint stamps and FDCs, but in the past special packs were produced either for the media or for presentation to government officials and other dignitaries. All of these things help to build the story of a stamp from its initial concept to the finished article.

plate proofs may consist of an entire sheet, a block or a strip. Single items will have very little margin as they are cut from the proof sheet.

Although die and plate proofs are normally pulled in black ink, they are often found in various colours to give postal officials the opportunity to select a shade most suitable for the finished stamp. These variations are regarded as colour trials and though they are usually imperforate they are sometimes perforated to give a better idea of what the finished stamp will look like. Both colour trials and examples of finished

Left: Specimen stamps from Germany, Cyprus and Taiwan.

Below: Pairs of New Zealand stamps (1926), in rejected and issued colours.

FLAWS AND MARGINAL MARKINGS

After narrowing the focus of a collection to take in the stamps and postal history of a particular country, period or theme, the logical next step for the ambitious philatelist is to create a study of the subtle minutiae of stamps from different printings or produced by different contractors. In order to do this successfully, it is necessary to employ tools and techniques which are far beyond those in general use.

TOOLS OF THE SPECIALIST

Instead of an ordinary perforation gauge, which measures quarter fractions, the advanced philatelist may rely on an electronic device such as the Perfotronic machine, which measures the gauge in tenths. While most collectors might be content to determine whether a stamp has one or two phosphor bands, or a single band on left or right, the specialist will want to distinguish between phosphor wavelengths and colour fluorescence, so a good ultraviolet lamp is essential.

LOOKING BENEATH THE SURFACE

Most collectors may be satisfied with sorting out different printings according to the watermark (as in the British Wilding definitives of 1955–67), but if you are studying the classic issues of the 19th century you will need to distinguish between wove and laid paper, hand- and machine-made paper, and

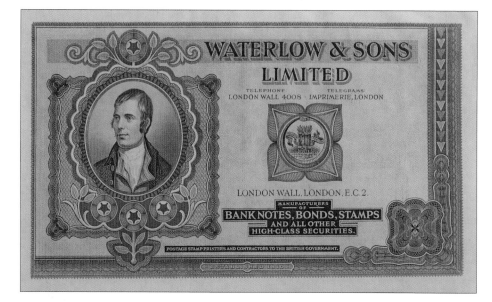

Above: The line-engraved trade card of Waterlow & Sons, printers of stamps and banknotes for much of the 19th and 20th centuries.

Right: US 37c stamp for the Athens Olympic Games, 2004, showing a marginal marking indicating the plate position. Other marginal markings include plate or cylinder numbers, printer's name and first date of sale.

even between different kinds of paper. Apart from the watermark detector you will need a micrometer to check the exact thickness of the paper and a really powerful illuminated magnifier to check the characteristics of the fibres that determine the quality or character of the paper.

In the period between the World Wars New Zealand had its stamps printed on paper supplied by different firms. Specialists therefore distinguish between De La Rue, Samuel Jones, Art, Cowan and Wiggins Teape papers. The wartime issues are known on first fine paper, second fine paper and coarse paper, further sub-divided according to whether the mesh of the paper is horizontal or vertical.

Some specialists end up spending all their time in the study of a single stamp. The Penny Black of 1840 and its eleven plates attract many specialists, but many albums could be filled with a detailed examination of the Penny Lilac (1881–1902), sometimes dubbed the Poor Man's Penny Black. The US George Washington 2c (1894–1900) and New Zealand's Penny Universal (1901–8) are also selected for study.

Wilding 2d Flaws

A constant flaw occurred in sideways coils of the Wilding 2d stamps from roll 5, the left hand numeral being very weak in the original printing. This weakness was rectified by retouching the figure but this, in turn, produced irregularities in its shape. The "retouched 2" remained constant in these coils, throughout changes from dark to light colour as well as changes of watermark.

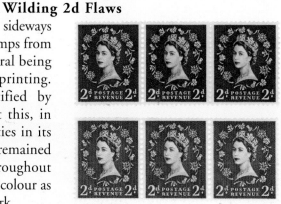

Above: The British Customs and Revenue Act of 1881 provided for stamps that served both postal and fiscal purposes. The Penny Lilac, inscribed "Postage and Inland Revenue", was widely used on bills and receipts as well as mail until 1902, providing a wealth of material for advanced study, hence its nickname: the Poor Man's Penny Black.

FLAWS AND VARIETIES

Apart from the inks, papers and processes that distinguish the work of one printer from another, the advanced collector must pay attention to the stamps themselves. Each printing method creates its own little quirks, resulting in minor blemishes in the stamps that are known to collectors as "flaws". They may be constant, appearing in the same plate or cylinder position throughout the print-run, such as the "screwdriver" flaws – white gashes caused by damage to the plates. Constant flaws help specialists to reconstruct entire sheets, a process known as "plating". Flaws may also be ephemeral, such as "confetti" flaws – patches of white on some stamps caused by small pieces of paper (often the fragments punched out by the perforators) adhering momentarily to the plate.

Weaknesses in line engraving can be corrected, causing a slight doubling of lines known as a "re-entry". Varieties in photogravure stamps can be corrected manually but the result is still obvious and is known as a "re-touch".

Flaws and varieties are best collected in positional blocks to show their relation to the sheet margins. Controls and cylinder blocks are generally kept in corner blocks of six (three by two) and arrow markings in blocks of four.

MARGINAL MARKINGS

Specialists are also preoccupied with the paper that surrounds sheets of stamps because of the useful information it contains. Back in 1840 the sheets of Penny Blacks included the plate number and instructions regarding the correct attachment of the stamp to the letter as well as the price per row (1s) or sheet (£1). From 1881 until 1947 British stamps bore a control letter alongside numerals indicating the last two digits of the year.

American and Canadian stamps had control numbers referring to the plates released to the printers. De La Rue stamps often had a numeral in a chamfered rectangle, the "current number", which indicated the order in which a plate was printed. Other sheet markings include arrows (to guide the counter clerks in dividing up the sheets in their stock), the printer's imprint or logo, and the exact date of printing.

Thick bars were inserted in the margins in 1887 to prevent wear on the plate. Known as "jubilee lines" (because they first appeared in the jubilee definitives of that year) they are a feature of British stamps to this day. Sheets of stamps in the early 20th century often had strange cuts in the jubilee lines, believed to be made by the printers to

Below: Part of a sheet of Welsh Scenery 43p stamps (2004) showing cylinder numbers, colour dabs and the sale date.

Above: A stamp from Israel's Ottoman Clock Tower series (2004) showing an accountancy mark in the right margin and a tab below.

identify certain plates. This feature sometimes forms part of the product description on sheets up for auction.

Modern offset litho and photogravure stamps have cylinder numbers in one margin and "traffic lights" (the printer's colour dabs) in the other. The stamps of many countries have the cumulative values of each row printed at the top or bottom to assist accounting. These "reckoning numbers" are not only helpful in plating but are often slightly changed and thus help to identify a particular printing.

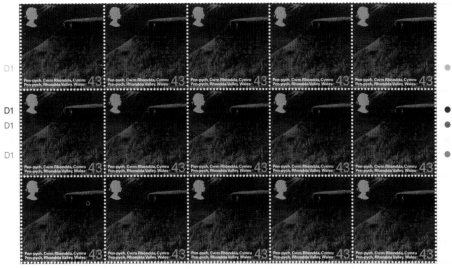

Sale Date   15-Jun-2004

A GLOBAL HOBBY

From its origins in the late 18th century, stamp collecting has emerged as the world's largest and most universal hobby. It is thought that more than 50 million people around the globe now collect, from crowned heads to schoolchildren.

THE ORIGINS OF THE HOBBY

Philately is an extremely interactive pastime, supported by a strong network of societies, magazines, study circles, websites, web-based discussion groups, and exhibitions of interest to both the amateur and the specialist. Some clubs, such as the Invalid and Lone Collectors Society in Britain, exist to establish links between collectors living in remote areas or who, perhaps due to ill health, lack the opportunity to meet others sharing their interest. For the serious collector, there are stamp auctions and dealers' bourses where the outstanding rarities have been known to change hands for seven-figure sums.

Below: Female postal workers examine love letters sent on St Valentine's Day. Despite frivolous portraits such as these, many 19th-century women took a serious interest in stamps, and some became avid pioneers of philately.

Left: A famous philatelic commemorative produced for an American-hosted exhibition of 1926.

EARLY COLLECTORS

Perhaps surprisingly, the earliest stamp collection was put together long before adhesive postage stamps (as we know them today) came into existence. As long ago as 1774, John Bourke, then Receiver-General of the Stamp Duties in Ireland, started a collection of revenue stamps, which had recently been introduced in that country. However, the father of stamp-collecting in the accepted sense was Dr John Edward Gray, Keeper of the Zoological Department of the British Museum. He took a very close interest in postal reform and was one of several people who later challenged Rowland Hill's claim to have invented stamps.

On the day the Penny Black went on sale (1 May 1840) Dr Gray purchased some examples of the stamp, which he kept as mementoes of a historic occasion. He subsequently added the Twopence Blue when it appeared on 8 May, and collected other stamps as soon as they were issued. In 1862 he was the compiler of one of the earliest stamp catalogues, and he also published sets of gummed titles, intended for collectors to cut up and use as headings for the pages of their stamp albums.

Apart from Dr Gray there must have been other men and women who were

Left and above: The first page of the inaugural issue of The Stamp Collector's Magazine, *February 1863, and a page advertising the sale of readers' stamps, labels and covers. for sale.*

quick to perceive the innate interest in these tiny scraps of paper and began forming collections of them. By 1850, when stamps from about 20 countries had appeared, and the number of issues in circulation had reached three figures, stamp collecting was well established as a hobby. As early as 1842 references to this strange new craze began to appear in newspaper and magazine articles. More significantly, advertisements of stamps wanted or for sale were being published by 1852. In that year a Belgian schoolmaster is said to have started encouraging his pupils to collect stamps, to improve their knowledge of geography.

Stanley Gibbons

Edward Stanley Gibbons was born in the same year as the Penny Black (1840) and began trading in stamps in 1856 from his father's shop in Plymouth, having purchased a collection of South African stamps from two sailors who had just returned to the port. Stamp trading apart, he led a colourful life, marrying five times.

THE FIRST DEALERS AND CATALOGUES

The hobby was certainly well established in Belgium by 1854, by which time Louis Hanciau and Jean-Baptiste Moens (who later became leading dealers) were avid enthusiasts. Edward Stanley Gibbons began dealing in stamps in 1856, a window of his father's pharmacy in Plymouth being devoted to mouth-watering bargains. Nine years later he published his first catalogue, the forerunner of the extensive range of general, specialized and thematic catalogues now on offer.

Oscar Berger-Levreult and Alfred Potiquet both began publishing catalogues in France in 1861 and not long afterwards there were regular magazines devoted to the hobby. One of the earliest was *The Stamp Collector's Magazine*, which first appeared in February 1863, and contained in its opening pages a very vivid account of the open-air selling and swapping of stamps conducted in Birchin Lane, Cheapside, in London, and the similar al fresco meetings of "timbromaniacs" held in the gardens of the Luxembourg and the Tuileries in Paris.

THE BIRTH OF PHILATELY

Timbromania, the original pseudo-scientific name for the hobby (from the French word *timbre*, a stamp), was soon replaced by something more dignified, if less easy to pronounce. Again it was a Frenchman, Georges Herpin, who coined the word "philately", but his logic was as faulty as his grasp of Greek. He tried to convey the idea of something on which no tax or charge was due because it was prepaid (*philos* = love, *a* = not, *telos* = tax), and thus ended up with a word that meant a lover of no taxes. Some have argued that "atelophily" would be more correct. Significantly, the Greeks themselves use the term *philotelia*, which omits the negative element, implying that stamp collectors are lovers of taxes rather than of the stamps that signify their payment.

FIRST STAMP CLUBS

Among the pioneer collectors was the Reverend F.J. Stainforth, who organized the first indoor meetings when the police began to discourage the obstruction caused in Birchin Lane. In the 1860s collectors met on Saturday afternoons in his rectory at All Hallows Staining in the City of London – its Dickensian ring is hardly surprising as it features in Dickens's novel *Dombey and Son*. The gatherings included Charles W. Viner, editor of *The Stamp Collector's Magazine*, Mount Brown, who published an early catalogue, Judge Philbrick and Sir Daniel Cooper, who became president of the Philatelic Society, London, when it was founded in 1869. A society had been formed in Paris in 1864 but it did not last long. The London society, now the Royal Philatelic Society, is still in existence and, if not the biggest, is certainly the most prestigious in the world.

Although stamp collecting is sometimes regarded as a male-dominated hobby, women have always played a prominent role in the field. Among the earliest female enthusiasts were Charlotte Tebay, who helped organize the earliest London exhibition, and Adelaide Lucy Fenton, who was a prolific contributor to the stamp magazines but, like some female novelists of an earlier generation, preferred to write under the masculine pen name of "Herbert Camoens".

The English school of philately was noted for its general approach, whereas the French school had a more scientific bent, paying greater attention to the minute variations in stamps. It was one of their number, Dr Jacques-Amable Legrand, who invented the perforation gauge in 1866 and wrote the earliest treatise on watermarks a year later.

Below: A society for young philatelists was, indeed, the brainchild of a young philatelist. Fred Melville was just 17 when he established the group in 1899, following his disappointment at being rejected as a member of the London Philatelic Society on account of his age. The first meeting is believed to have been held in a shop in Clapham, South London, and the Junior Philatelic Society went on to become the National Philatelic Society, which celebrated its centenary in 1999.

ORGANIZED PHILATELY

Stamp collecting endured a sticky patch in the 1870s (*The Stamp Collector's Magazine* ceased publication in 1874, and its rival *The Philatelist* in 1876, for lack of support), but somehow it managed to keep going and steadily gained ground in the 1880s. By then it was well established throughout Europe and North America, with numerous dealers and stamp auctions.

GROWTH OF STAMP CLUBS

The reason for the loss of interest in the 1870s was probably the paucity of stamp clubs; without the interaction of fellow enthusiasts, many of the original collectors lost heart and gave up. The resurgence of the hobby began in continental Europe, where a national philatelic society was revived in France at the end of 1875.

A stamp club had started in New York in 1867 but soon faded into oblivion and it was not until 1886 that the American Philatelic Society (APS) was formed. Chartered by Congress in 1912, it is now the world's largest stamp club, with its headquarters and magnificent library in State College, Pennsylvania. About the same time the Manchester Philatelic Society was established in England. The Edinburgh & Leith Philatelic Society, founded in 1890, was almost entirely composed of expatriate German businessmen and for the first three years the minutes were recorded in German. By the beginning of the 20th century there were 34 philatelic societies in the UK, a score in the British colonies, a dozen in the USA, 19 in continental Europe and nine in Latin America.

EARLY STAMP EXHIBITIONS

In 1887 the first stamp exhibition took place at Antwerp. Two years later similar shows were organized in New York, Amsterdam and Munich. In 1890 – the golden jubilee of adhesive postage stamps – exhibitions were staged in Vienna, Birmingham, Edinburgh and Leeds as well as London (for which some of the earliest special postmarks were produced). Undoubtedly such exhibitions attracted the general public and drew many new recruits.

Below: The American Philatelic Society, established in 1886 as the American Philatelic Association, has hosted annual conventions for many years.

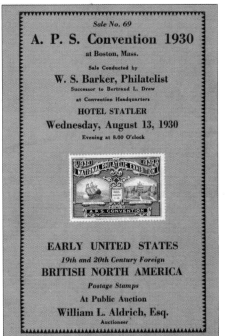

World Fair Stamps

New York's fair of technology and science, held from 1939 to 1940, brought hope to an era of international tension. A commemorative stamp was issued by the USPO in the Fair's first year. Some participating countries, such as Iceland, issued postage stamps to fund their attendance at the two-year global exhibition. The Centennial Stamp Exhibition was one of many around the world that marked the centenary of the Penny Black.

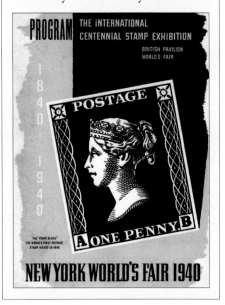

Philatelic literature, including handbooks and monographs as well as general catalogues, had grown to such an extent that, by 1889, the Munich exhibition included more than 500 volumes. The first exhibition devoted to stamps of particular countries took place in 1893 when the Philatelic Society of London staged a show of British India, Ceylon and the West Indies. The Society's exhibition the following year was dedicated to rare stamps in general.

The first London exhibition in 1890 had been a major landmark. Although the centenary exhibition in 1940 was muted as a result of the outbreak of World War II, it set the precedent for

Above: The label for the Centenary International Philatelic Exhibition, New York, 1947, celebrating the centenary of the first US stamps.

Below: A souvenir sheet for the London International Stamp Exhibition, 1960, portraying Colonel Henry Bishop and the many different "Bishop marks" used by staff to record acceptance of mail from the 1660s to the late 18th century.

the great international shows that have been held in London at ten-year intervals ever since.

NATIONAL CONGRESSES AND REGIONAL FEDERATIONS

The Philatelic Congress of Great Britain was inaugurated at Manchester in 1909 as an opportunity for fellow collectors to meet and discuss the hobby. It has been held annually ever since, with the exception of the war years, in different venues, and has generated sufficient material, in the form of souvenir covers, postcards, labels, miniature sheets and postmarks, to make a sizeable collection.

With the proliferation of stamp clubs after World War II, an intermediate tier of organization was created in Britain, with federations of clubs at county or regional level but including national associations in Scotland, Wales and Northern Ireland, all coming under the aegis of the Association of British Philatelic Societies. Similar federations at state or provincial level exist in the USA and Canada and the great majority of countries in the rest of Europe, Australasia and Latin America.

Major international exhibitions are now held several times a year in different parts of the world. The governing body is the Fédération Internationale de Philatélie (FIP), which sets out the rules for competitions and judging. It also attempts to apply the brake on excessive and unnecessary stamp issues. This is a perennial problem that has so far defeated the continuing efforts of the Universal Postal Union and the International Federation of Stamp Dealers' Associations (IFDSA).

Below: The Junior Philatelic Society of the United Kingdom organized a number of national exhibitions during the first half of the 20th century. Due to a falling-out between the London and Manchester branches, the 1909 exhibition held at the latter failed to draw any mention from the society's journal, Stamp Lover.

CLUBS AT LOCAL AND NATIONAL LEVEL

Most towns of any size now boast at least one stamp club, meeting monthly or more frequently, where collectors can exchange unwanted duplicates, buy and sell stamps and attend talks and displays by prominent philatelists.

In recent years, specialist society or study groups have emerged, drawing together collectors of similar interests and specialization at national or even international level. Although these societies hold regular meetings, the main medium for intercourse is the club magazine, in which new research is published, and nowadays most if not all of these specialist organizations have excellent websites. Most clubs, at both local and national level, also maintain a club "packet" – a system that enables all members to add to their collections with the minimum of expense.

Below: In October 1926, first day covers were issued at the International Philatelic Exhibition for the very first time. Although FDCs with 16 October 1926 date stamps are known, this is widely regarded as an error. It is now believed the postal clerk simply forgot to change the date stamp as stamps were officially issued on 18 October.

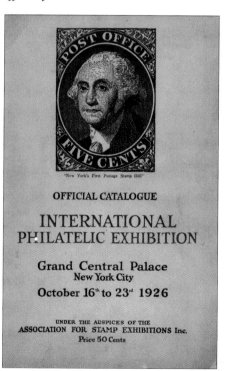

EXHIBITING STAMPS

Stamp exhibitions have been around for almost 120 years and during that time they have changed from being confined purely to competitive and invited displays by private individuals to becoming the great crossroads of philately, where dealers and philatelic bureaux congregate and collectors flock from all over the world to examine their merchandise.

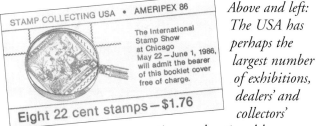

Purists may decry this trend and feel that the stamp displays have been relegated to a secondary role. The British Philatelic Exhibition (BPE) was, in fact, established as a rival to Stampex (the other major British national show) to try to return to a situation where stamp displays were the main attraction of the event. However, the organizers were forced to admit the dealers' stands at subsequent shows because their absence meant that attendance figures slumped. In the 1970s Stampex was held in February or March and BPE in October or November. Nowadays,

Above and left: The USA has perhaps the largest number of exhibitions, dealers' and collectors' conventions and national bourses, many of which attract collectors from all over the world.

Below: The US-hosted International Philatelic Exhibitions provided good opportunities to promote the sale of souvenir sheets or new commemoratives.

both shows are organized under the aegis of the Philatelic Traders' Society (PTS) and are known as the Spring and Autumn Stampex. In turn, they now have a rival in the form of Philatex, which is held more or less simultaneously, with a bias towards postal history.

EXHIBITIONS AT ALL LEVELS
There are numerous regional exhibitions and conventions in Britain, usually organized by the federations of philatelic societies. These shows tend to lay more emphasis on competitive displays, though dealers' stands are also a major attraction. A similar pattern is to be found in other countries.

The USA leads the way in organizing philatelic exhibitions, but they are also staged each year at club, regional and national level all over Europe, Australasia and an ever-increasing number of countries in the Third World. The most phenomenal growth in recent years has taken place in Singapore, Hong Kong and the People's Republic of China. The annual stamp shows in Beijing and Shanghai, for example, attract crowds in excess of 300,000 – an astronomical attendance. Six-figure attendance has also been recorded at exhibitions in Prague,

Above: Philatelic exhibitions occur throughout the world each year. This event was hosted in Helsinki, Finland.

Budapest, Warsaw and other capital cities that, not so long ago, were suffering from numerous restrictions under communist rule.

Many countries have a national stamp day, stamp week or even stamp month, when their postal administrations collaborate with the trade bodies to promote the hobby by means of exhibitions. Sales of special stamps for these events go a long way in subsidizing the shows.

ENTERING COMPETITIVE SHOWS
Those who aspire to take part in the competitive sections of the international exhibitions must first earn a silver medal or a higher award at national level: this ensures that the standards of the entries in the main annual exhibitions are kept high. To attain this level may take many years of competing at a local club show, gradually improving the layout and writing-up of the display, and acquiring those philatelic gems that make all the difference between the mediocre and the first-rate, till the collection is ready for the big national

shows. The coveted silver medal, however, is no more than the key to the door of the most prestigious events, and such an entry at international exhibitions may receive only a certificate of participation at the first attempt.

Such is the competitive instinct in many stamp collectors that initial disappointment will merely spur them on to greater efforts, and over the years they will climb the ladder of international awards from bronze and bronze-silver medals, through silver, silver-gilt or vermeil awards to small and large gold medals. At the pinnacle of the awards system are the national and international Grand Prix and the special trophies in each class. Thereafter the Grand Prix winners may be invited to exhibit *hors concours* (out of contest) in the Court of Honour, alongside exhibits from the world's most prestigious stamp collections, such as those belonging to Queen Elizabeth II or Prince Rainier of Monaco.

It is when you see these dazzling arrays of the great rarities that you appreciate the old adage about stamp collecting being "the king of hobbies and the hobby of kings", although today's biggest collectors are more likely to be property tycoons, industrial millionaires, film stars and pop idols, while the greatest rarities are probably owned by investment syndicates and union pension funds.

However, stamp collecting is still primarily the hobby of countless millions of ordinary men, women and children all over the world, and it is with them that its enduring strength lies. These are the collectors who are the mainstay of the exhibitions, preparing their competition entries of 16 or 32 sheets (the minimum basic requirement at regional level) or multiple frames of 16 sheets at national and international level.

Below: Promotional stamps and stationery are often produced in conjunction with exhibitions and national stamp centenaries or commemorative dates introduced to plug the hobby.

Above: Large stamp exhibitions have often attracted people of note, including royalty and politicians. At this British exhibition during the 1950s the future prime minister, Harold Wilson, examines Cape Triangular stamps.

FIP MARKING SYSTEM

Under the rules of the Fédération Internationale de Philatélie, entries are given marks for presentation, philatelic material, philatelic treatment and philatelic knowledge. Presentation covers overall appearance, including marks for the title page, which should act as an index to the display itself. Material deals with the stamps and other items, their quality and rarity, while treatment pertains to the ways in which they are set out. Philatelic knowledge accounts for a third of the marks, and this is where exhibitors can really shine by demonstrating their original research. But you must study the rules carefully to make sure that you do not include anything that will detract from the display and lose you marks that might mean all the difference between a gold and silver medal.

Competitive Philately

Records held by the National Philatelic Society of the United Kingdom help to characterize competitive philately during the 1920s. The Society's first International Stamp Exhibition was held in London in 1923, and planning began at least two years before. There was a design competition for "Air Post Stamps", with premiums of twenty and ten guineas (£21 and £10.50) for the two best entrants. The American millionaire collector Arthur Hind exhibited his rare Mauritius 1d and 2d values and there was even an early nod to thematic and Cinderella collecting in competitive categories such as "War and Post-War Stamps" and "Etceteras", the latter including displays of proofs, essays, specimens, errors, forgeries, embossed stamps, Mulready envelopes and Chinese treaty port material.

BUYING AND SELLING STAMPS

Although it is possible to collect stamps with little or no outlay, concentrating on the stamps off your mail, sooner or later you are going to have to buy material if you are to make any real headway in the hobby. There are four main methods of acquiring stamps by purchase: from other collectors, from a dealer, from an auction and direct from a post office counter or philatelic bureau. The first three outlets are also useful for disposing of stamps.

GRADE AND CONDITION

Before you start trading it is worth understanding the principles behind grade and condition if you want to be able to calculate the approximate value of a stamp.

The "grade" of a stamp is determined by the actual position of the printed design on the paper, in relation to the perforated edges. The relative imprecision of perforating methods in the past means that the "margins" (the area of unprinted paper surrounding the printed design) of many older stamps vary considerably in width. Stamps with larger margins tend to attract collectors more than examples where the design is tight against the

Below: Collectors browse through booklets of stamps available for sale at the bourse of a large stamp show.

edges. Grading in catalogues such as Gibbons or Scott uses terms such as "fair", "good", "fine", "very fine", and so on. It is generally assumed that if the stamp has a balanced appearance and the design is well clear of the edges, it counts for a "fine" or "very fine" grade. Imperforate stamps should present three normal-size margins.

"Condition" is based on a greater number of factors: the effects of production, whether the stamp is hinged, the nature of the cancellation on a used stamp, or any evidence of damage (such as missing perforated "teeth", tears or faded colour due to prolonged exposure to sunlight). Of course, the grade of the stamp can also affect its condition. All of the above may detract from a stamp's commercial value, although some of the more quirky or historically weighty cancellations may render some used issues highly sought after by collectors.

TRADING WITH OTHER COLLECTORS

You can buy, sell or swap stamps with other collectors at a stamp club, either face to face or through the medium of the club exchange packet or "circuit". This usually consists of a box containing a quantity of small booklets with stamps, cards and covers mounted on their pages, with the prices clearly marked. Trading circuits organized by societies such as the APS have designated sales books, and even specific mounts for displaying material, but the principle remains the same. In most cases it is customary also to add the catalogue number with the catalogue price (for mint or used).

When trading among themselves, collectors generally work on a quarter to a fifth of the catalogue price, a basis that allows you to add to your collection with the minimum of expense. This may not seem like a good deal from the vendor's viewpoint, but it probably amounts to a more generous

percentage than is obtained by selling to a dealer. The only snags about selling through the club packet are that it is time-consuming to mount and price stamps individually (although many collectors actually enjoy this) and, of course, many months may elapse before the packet has been around everyone on the circuit and you get back the (hopefully) empty booklets with a tidy sum of cash, less the modest commission due to the club funds.

DEALERS

Even stamp dealers usually offer material at a discount off the catalogue price, although if the stamps are particularly elusive you should be prepared to pay over the odds sometimes. Catalogue prices are usually a fair indication of relative value, but occasionally even these are at odds with reality. While in some (though not all) cases the catalogue represents the selling price of a major dealer, that dealer may be deliberately keeping prices low (when, for example, the company wishes to buy material for stock). Other dealers recognize this and will often ignore the standard catalogue and fix their own price, based on what they had to pay at auction.

If you decide to sell to a dealer you may be in for quite a shock. What he offers you may be only a fifth of what you paid – sometimes less – especially if you are trading in your entire collection rather than selected items. The reason for this large differential between buying and selling price is mainly economic. When appraising a collection, dealers ignore all the common stamps (of which they will already have a large stock that is slow to turn over) and will base their valuation on the scarcer or more expensive individual items. Selling stamps this way, however, means that you get cash on the spot – useful if you need money in a hurry.

FINDING THE RIGHT DEALER

For every dealer with a retail shop there are probably 100 whose business is postal or by appointment only. Some of the world's largest dealers operate in quite a modest manner, acting on behalf of a few very wealthy clients who will regularly spend large sums with them. They are truly international, traversing the world in search of major rarities, relying on their laptops, bidding at auctions online and emailing clients to set up new deals.

At the other end of the scale are the vast majority of dealers, who are content to make a modest living, meeting potential customers on the fair circuits, which have now largely superseded the retail shops. Others have found niches specializing in certain countries or types of material, sending out price lists to regular clients and laboriously making up approval booklets in which stamps and covers are mounted and priced.

Apart from the excellent directories of dealers published by such bodies as the American Stamp Dealers' Association (ASDA) and the Philatelic Traders' Society (PTS) in Britain, the easiest way to contact a dealer specializing in your field is to scour the classified advertisements in the philatelic magazines. If yours is a popular subject the choice of dealers will be bewildering, but whatever your interests – no matter how esoteric – somewhere there will be at least one dealer specializing in them. As a rule, the dealers with a retail shop tend to hold general stocks as they have to cater to all tastes, whereas the postal dealers are more likely to concentrate on specific subjects. Many of them are leading authorities in their chosen speciality and you can usually rely on their judgment and integrity.

AUCTIONS

The stamp auction is where the best stamps and postal history material come up for sale, and this is where you are most likely to find entire collections and specialized studies that can form the basis for further expansion, as well as the more choice single items that fill that long-felt want.

If you attend a sale, make sure you know before it begins what your spending limit is, and stick to it. Too often, a couple of bidders get carried away in their reckless attempt to secure a coveted item and one ends up paying well over the odds. You also need to remember that most auctions nowadays charge a buyer's premium (usually 15 per cent) and that a general consumer tax may be payable on that, so the net sum you have to fork out on a purchase could turn out to be substantially more than your final bid.

It is also possible to place your bid by post. In this case you need to state the maximum you are prepared to pay on each lot and the auctioneer will let you have it at the next step above the highest room bid or the next highest postal bid to yours.

If you have good material to dispose of, selling at auction offers the best method of ensuring the maximum return, but bear in mind that the auctioneer takes a percentage of the sum realized, and many months may elapse between sending stamps to the auction and the sale itself, as material has to be appraised, lotted and described, catalogues printed and dispatched to prospective bidders, and then all the paperwork after the sale completed before you receive a remittance.

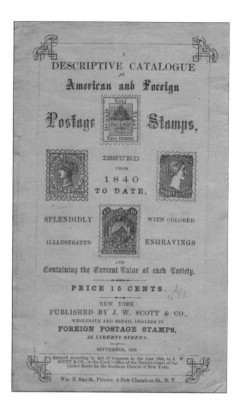

Above: An early auction catalogue. The first auction devoted entirely to stamps was held in Paris in 1865. Five years later, the American philatelist J. Walter Scott (founder of the Scott philatelic empire) organized his first sale in New York, and by the 1880s stamp auctions were a regular occurrence, with firms established solely to generate philatelic sales. Although London was dominant for many years, today there are many excellent stamp auctions in Geneva, Sydney, Singapore and Hong Kong.

PHILATELIC BUREAUX

Virtually every national postal administration now operates a philatelic bureau, selling stamps, postal stationery, FDCs and other products direct to collectors, and all transactions can be made by credit card. You pay only face value for your purchases, plus a small handing charge in many cases, but this ensures you get everything relevant to your chosen country, and sometimes a bonus such as a proof or special print unavailable across the post office counter. Bureaux produce annual catalogues of back stock as well as their own magazines, usually quarterly, announcing forthcoming issues, often with excellent background stories.

PHILATELY ONLINE

We are living in the heart of an IT revolution that impacts on every aspect of our lives, from split-second global communications to online shopping and banking, and information retrieval. Stamp collecting is also currently being transformed by the advent of the internet, with countless societies, clubs, magazines, dealers, auctioneers and centres of research offering online facilities to assist in the expansion and refinement of collections.

In addition to the ever-growing number of internet research outlets, there are also numerous software packages that assist the collector with everything from forming an inventory to calculating the value of stamps or downloading pre-designed album pages. Magazines, journals and societies often publish reviews of the latest philatelic software, and their merits (or pitfalls) are regularly debated in online discussion forums – which are themselves one of the fastest-growing

France C22 (StampID: 403350831)

Air Mail, L H, Bird, VF-XF

Condition: Unused, H
Cover: Year: 1900-1940
Other Cat Name: Other Cat #:

Catalog Value: $42.50

Sale Price: $31.29

+ Add to Cart   E-Mail To Friend

Q Zoom   ‹ Back to Search   ? Ask a Question

Above: Some of the larger philatelic societies offer a rigorously organized form of online "club packet", which enables members to swap stamps and even submit queries about a purchase.

Viewing Stamps Online

Stamps for sale on the internet are often accompanied by digital images of such quality that it is possible to discern individual fibres in the paper and verify the distance between the perforations. This Bavarian stamp displays a number of missing, or "pulled", perfs, which can affect value.

resources available to the online philatelic fraternity. Another hotly debated topic is the advantages or disadvantages of purchasing stamps online, which is becoming an increasingly popular alternative to local, face-to-face dealing.

RESEARCH AT THE CLICK OF A MOUSE

One of the biggest problems facing the thematic or topical collector is finding out about the subjects of stamps. The basic details such as the reason for the issue are given in stamp catalogues, but for a topical collection you often need to get the whole story – the why and the wherefore as well as the hidden meaning. It is ferreting out such information that gains good marks in competitive displays.

This is where search engines such as Google and Yahoo come into their own. There is, seemingly, absolutely nothing under the sun that cannot be found in this way, providing you type in a clear and concise phrase rather than a single keyword, which might yield far more than you require, much of it irrelevant. The search engines are also invaluable for researching postal history, and can help you to locate masses of information on the places whose postmarks you are interested in, as well as simply drawing your attention to organizations that can help

further. Long-established thematic societies, such as the American Topical Association, also have their own websites, with useful tips and links for the keen researcher.

DATABASES, INVENTORIES AND WANTS LISTS

Stamp catalogues remain key to the process of identifying and valuing individual issues or long-running series. Yet there exists an increasing demand among collectors to be able to tailor these set-format reference tools to meet their individual needs. Some of the biggest catalogue publishers, such as Scott, are now working in conjunction with philatelic software producers to combine the entire catalogue of a country with the benefits of a personal inventory, so that a collector can itemize their prized possessions and identify gaps in their collection.

The idea is that the collector will not only be able to sort and display stamps by numerous categories, such as catalogue number and issue date, but also use the software to generate a personal record of their own collection.

Current software offers the opportunity to revise information on value, add further details on format, grade and condition, and even upload digital scans. The best packages offer considerable space for editing data on each stamp – sometimes up to one page per issue. The collector can also inventory reports, calculate the value of a bulk of stamps, and generate wants lists to mail to dealers and other collectors.

Some of this software can be downloaded direct from the supplier's website, although before purchasing it is worth checking that the dealer is reputable and that a full mailing address, with customer service contact, is given. There may be free trial downloads, so that you can check that you are happy with the format of the software before purchasing it.

BUYING AND SELLING ONLINE

The ability to trade online is probably the most significant part of the internet revolution in stamp collecting. Stamp dealers who scraped a bare living catering to customers living in their neighbourhood have now found that by creating their own website their stock is available to the world at large. Collectors have found thousands of dealers and auctioneers, large and small, general and specialized, whose wares are to be found simply by clicking on to their websites. Most philatelic bureaux have also embraced this technology and it has become a very simple matter to select what you want and pay for it by credit card.

Apart from the various auctioneers, who also have websites nowadays and enable you to bid online, there are larger, less esoteric organizations such as Ebay, where online sales are in continuous operation. Nor does buying online always require putting in a bid. In America, *Linn's Stamp News* runs a site at www.zillionsofstamps.com – open to all – that gives the collector the opportunity to input data on a wanted stamp and then search by dealer. The American Philatelic Society runs its own stamps store for members at

www.stampstore.org, where the collector can browse stamps, selecting them by keyword, catalogue number, country or even type, such as "air mails". APS members can also submit information on stamps they wish to sell to other collectors.

For all forms of buying and selling, the computer scores heavily because it is now possible to download high-resolution images of stamps, which make even the most sumptuous of printed catalogues look crude by comparison. Fakes (stamps that have been tampered with to improve their appearance or altered by cleaning off the cancellation to convert a cheap used stamp into a valuable mint one) are no longer such a headache for potential buyers, because high-resolution images of stamps will immediately show up any imperfection, repair or other signs of alteration.

DISCUSSION FORUMS

One of the latest developments in this interactive hobby is for collectors to meet and chat with fellow enthusiasts from anywhere in the world via online messaging services. This can be done by posting notices to message boards,

or by participating in a "live" discussion. Many philatelic forums have countless discussions running at any one time – on every subject from catalogue prices to the latest commemoratives, how to get started in collecting or experiences of online auction bidding. A code of conduct is usually encouraged during these discussions – namely that the participants stick to the subject at hand. Two of the busiest stamp collector forums, with spirited discussions, are the Virtual Stamp Club (www.virtualstampclub.com) and Frajola's Board for Philatelists (www.rfrajola.com). These sites also offer other standard facilities such as a bookstore and archive search facility.

Below: Global auction sites such as Ebay have embraced online philatelic trading. The number of bids is often displayed in a "counter" at the bottom of the screen. If you are not too familiar with the stamps you are bidding for, check that the seller has included their catalogue value with the lot, otherwise you may end up paying over the odds. Before getting involved in a bidding war, determine the maximum amount you wish to pay per stamp.

USEFUL SERVICES AND ADDRESSES

For the vast majority of collectors the standard stamp catalogues, published by long-established firms such as Gibbons (UK), Scott (USA), Michel (Germany) or Yvert et Tellier (France), are their bibles. The more advanced collectors are not content with one or other of the great general catalogues but require the specialized catalogues of their chosen countries – which may entail learning a foreign language as the best of the detailed catalogues, monographs and other reference works tend to be confined to the language of the country under study.

RESEARCHING THE MACHINS

The following example may help to illustrate the difference between the different levels of catalogues. The Machin decimal definitives of the UK, launched in 1971 and still going strong, occupy a column in the Gibbons *Stamps of the World* (2004 edition), which lists 120 stamps by denomination and colour only. The same stamps, classified by printer, printing process, perforation and phosphor, occupy nine columns in the Gibbons *British Commonwealth* volume 1, while volume 4 of the *Specialised Stamp Catalogue*, devoted entirely to the decimal definitives, now runs to almost 950 pages. This catalogue explains the differences in the stamps produced by Harrison, Enschedé, Questa and De La Rue (photogravure), Questa, Waddington and Walsall (lithography) and Bradbury

Wilkinson, Enschedé or De La Rue (intaglio). It details the variations in the queen's effigy (high or

Left: Three British second class Machin definitives, printed by Walsall, Harrison and Questa, can be identified by the sheet markings.

low), whether chemically etched or computer engraved, and distinguishes the numerous types of paper, gum, perforation (normal or elliptical in different gauges), cylinder varieties, marginal markings, booklets and coils.

Many advanced collectors prefer the *Complete Deegam Machin Handbook* compiled by Douglas Myall, who is also the author of the *Deegam Catalogue of Machin Se-tenant Pairs* and even a catalogue of *Elizabethan Coil Leaders*. Beyond that, an absolute must is membership of the Great Britain Philatelic Society, which has a separate Machin chapter, or the Decimal Book Study Circle, which publishes *The Bookmark* detailing the latest research by members. In fact, it is the pooling of information by individual collectors, who devote a considerable amount of time and money to researching the latest printings, that helps to maintain the extraordinary momentum of interest in this series.

CHECKING PREVIOUS RESEARCH

There is a vast literature on all aspects of philately and postal history, from monumental treatises running to several volumes, to articles in general and specialist magazines. A great deal of research by countless students into the most subtle minutiae of stamps and more esoteric aspects of postal history is to be found. Much of it has probably never been distilled and published in even the advanced catalogues. One task for the collector researching their material in detail is to find out what has already been published on the subject; sourcing all this secondary material takes quite a lot of research in itself.

MUSEUMS AND ARCHIVES

Many countries have at least one museum devoted to philately. In the USA the Smithsonian Institution in Washington has one of the world's largest philatelic collections, or rather

a whole host of different collections pertaining to stamps, from a general whole-world reference collection to specialized studies and a wealth of postal history material. There are excellent facilities for studying these collections. The American Philatelic Society's extensive premises in State

---

Which Catalogue?

The following is an alphabetical list of the geographical areas covered by the key stamp catalogue producers. Although some of the larger publishers, such as Gibbons and Scott, also produce "world guides", they are listed here according to the country of which they have the most extensive coverage.

Australian Commonwealth Specialized Australia
AAMS US and Canadian Air Mail Covers
Bale Israel/Palestine
Barefoot European Revenues and British Revenues
Brookman United States
Campbell-Paterson New Zealand
Higgins & Gage Global Postal Stationery (10 yr)
Michel Germany
Minkus/Krause United States, Canada and United Nations
Nederlandsche (NVPH) Netherlands
Sanabria Airmail Catalogue Global Air Mail stamps (10 yr)
Sassone Italy
Scott United States
Springer Handbooks Non-Scott-listed US Revenues
Stanley Gibbons Great Britain
Steven's Mexican Revenues (10 yr)
Unitrade Canada and Provinces
World Perfin Catalogue Worldwide (printed in sections)
Yvert-Tellier France
Zumstein Switzerland

College, Pennsylvania also has some amazing reference collections, often donated or bequeathed by members, but its strong point is its library – one of the finest in the world.

At the other end of the spectrum is the National Postal Museum in London. This was located in the old General Post Office in the very heart of the City, but since the Post Office sold the building for redevelopment the museum has been in storage, under the management of the Post Office Heritage Collections. In the country that invented stamps and did so much to develop postal services this is a scandal of international proportions. The British Library is home to the Tapling Collection, containing many of the world's greatest rarities, as well as many other collections, available for research.

Elsewhere in the world, from Paris to Pretoria, there are postal museums and archives crammed with source material. The following associations may be able to offer advice on how to broaden the scope of your study.

Philatelic Societies

American Philatelic Society
100 Match Factory Place, Bellefonte, PA 16875, USA, www.stamps.org (*The American Philatelist, Philatelic Literature Review*)

American Poster Stamp Society
3654 Applegate Road, Jacksonville, OR 97530, USA

American Topical Association
PO Box 50820, Albuquerque, NM 87181-0820, USA (*Topical Time*)

Australian Philatelic Federation Ltd, PO Box 829, South Melbourne BC VIC 3205, Australia

British Philatelic Centre
107 Charterhouse Street, London EC1M 6PT, UK, www.ukphilately.org.uk
    Association of British Philatelic Societies
    British Philatelic Trust
    National Philatelic Society (*Stamp Lover*)

The Philatelic Traders' Society Limited, PO Box 371, Fleet, Hampshire GU52 6ZX

Right: The American Philatelic Research Library, based at the APS premises in Bellefonte, Pennsylvania, is the largest public philatelic library in the United States. It houses classic periodicals and catalogues, and is open to the general public.

The Cinderella Stamp Club
www.cinderellastampclub.org.uk
(*The Cinderella Philatelist*)

Collectors Club of New York
22 East 35 Street, New York, NY 100016-3806, USA, www.collectorsclub.org
(*The Collectors Club Philatelist*)

The Ephemera Society of America, Inc.
PO Box 95, Cazenovia, NY 13035-0095, www.ephemerasociety.org (*Ephemera Journal*)

Invalid and Lone Collectors Club
12 Appian Close, Kings Heath, Birmingham, B14 6DS, UK

Philatelic Foundation
21 East 40th Street, New York, NY 100016, USA

Royal Philatelic Society
41 Devonshire Place, London W1N 1PE, UK, www.rpsl.org.uk (*The London Philatelist*)

Philatelic Magazines
Canadian Stamp News
Trajan Publications, 103 Lakeshore Road, Suite 202, St Catharines, Ontario L2N 2T6, Canada, www.trajan.ca

Gibbons Stamp Monthly
5 Parkside, Christchurch Road, Ringwood, Hampshire BH24 3SH, UK
www.gibbonsstampmonthly.com

Right: The Bath Postal Museum, England, is situated in the building from which one of the first letters bearing a Penny Black was sent on 2 May 1840 – four days ahead of the official date.

Global Stamp News
PO Box 97, Sidney, OH 45365-0097, USA

Linn's Stamp News
PO Box 29, 911 Vandemark Road, Sidney, OH 45365-0065, USA, www.linns.com

The Philatelic Exporter
PO Box 137, Hatfield, Hertfordshire, AL10 9DB, UK, www.philatelicexporter.com

Scott Stamp Monthly
PO Box 828, Sidney, OH 45365, USA, www.scottonline.com

Stamp and Coin Mart
Trinity Publications Ltd, Edward House, 92–3 Edward Street, Birmingham, B1 2RA, UK, www.stampmart.co.uk

Stamp Collector
700 East State Street, Iola, WI 54990-0001, USA, www.krause.com

Stamp Magazine
IPC Media, Leon House, 233 High Street, Croydon CR9 1HZ, UK, www.stampmagazine.co.uk

Stamp News
PO Box 1410, Dubbo, NSW 3830, Australia

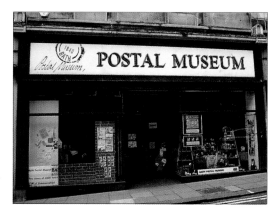

INSCRIPTIONS

Most stamps can be identified by their inscription, language and expressions of value, but there are some that baffle even the collector of long standing. Below is a list of key-words and abbreviations found in inscriptions and overprints, with their country, state or district of origin.

A & T Annam and Tonquin
Acores Azores
Afghanes Afghanistan
Africa Portuguese Africa
Akahi Keneta Hawaii
Amtlicher Verkehr Württemberg
AO (Afrika Ost) Ruanda-Urundi
Allemagne/Duitschland Belgian occupation of Germany
A Payer Te Betalen Belgium (postage due)
A Percevoir postage due Belgium (francs and centimes); Egypt (paras, milliemes)
Archipel des Comores Comoro Islands
Avisporto Denmark
Azad Hind Free India (unissued stamps prepared for use in India after Japanese "liberation")
B (on Straits Settlements) Bangkok
Bani (on Austrian stamps) Austrian occupation of Romania
BATYM Batum (now Batumi)
Bayer, Bayern Bavaria

BCA British Central Africa (now Malawi)
Belgique/Belgie/Belgien, also **Belge** Belgium
Böhmen und Mahren Bohemia and Moravia
Bollo delta Posta Napoletana Naples
Bosnien Bosnia
Braunschweig Brunswick
C CH Cochin China
Cechy a Morava Bohemia and Moravia
CEF (on India) Chinese Expeditionary Force
CEF (on German colonies) Cameroons under British occupation
Centesimi (on Austria) Austrian occupation of Italy
Centimes (on Austria) Austrian POs in Crete
Centrafricaine Central African Republic
Ceskoslovensko Czechoslovakia
Chiffre taxe France
Chine French POs in China
Comunicaciones Spain
Confed. Granadina Granadine Confederation (Colombia)
Cong Hoa Mien Nam National Liberation Front for South Vietnam
Congo Belge Belgian Congo
Continente Portuguese mainland
Coree Korea
Correio Brazil, Portugal
Correos Spain, Cuba, Porto Rico, Philippines
Côte d'Ivoire Ivory Coast

Côte Française des Somalis French Somali Coast
Danmark Denmark
Dansk Vestindien Danish West Indies
DDR German Democratic Republic
Deficit Peru
Deutsch Neu-Guinea German New Guinea
Deutsch Ostafrika German East Africa
Deutschösterreich Austria
Deutsch Südwestafrika German South West Africa
Deutsche Flugpost/ Reichspost Germany
Deutsches Reich Germany
Dienstmarke Germany
Dienstsache Germany
Diligencia Uruguay
DJ Djibouti
Drzava, Drzavna Yugoslavia
EEF Palestine
Eesti Estonia
EE UU de C Colombia
EFO French Oceania
Eire Republic of Ireland
Elua Keneta Hawaii
Emp. Franc. French Empire
Emp. Ottoman Turkey
Equateur Ecuador
Escuelas Venezuela
España, Espanola Spain
Estados Unidos de Nueva Granada Colombia
Estensi Modena
Estero Italian POs in the Levant
Etablissements de l'Inde French Indian Settlements

Etablissements de l'Océanie French Oceanic Settlements
Etat Ind. du Congo Congo Free State
Filipinas Spanish Philippines
Franco Switzerland
Francobollo Italy
Franco Marke Bremen
Franco Poste Bollo Neapolitan provinces and early Italy
Franqueo Peru
Franquicia Postal Spain
Freimarke Württemberg, Prussia
Frimerke Norway
Frimaerke Denmark
G (on Cape of Good Hope) Griqualand West
G & D Guadeloupe
GEA Tanganyika
Gen. Gouv. Warschau German occupation of Poland, World War 1
General Gouvernement German occupation of Poland, World War II
Georgie Georgia
Giuba Jubaland
GPE Guadeloupe
GRI British occupation of New Guinea and Samoa
Grossdeutsches Reich Nazi Germany
Guine Portuguese Guinea
Guinea Ecuatorial Equatorial Guinea
Guiné French Guinea
Gultig 9 Armee German occupation of Romania
Guyane Française French Guiana
Haute Volta Upper Volta
Hellas Greece
Helvetia Switzerland
HH Nawab Shah Begam Bhopal

Hrvatska Croatia
HRZGL Holstein
IEF Indian Expeditionary Force
IEF 'D' Mosul
Imper. Reg. Austrian POs in Turkey
Impuesto de Guerra Spain (war tax)
Inde French Indian Settlements
India Port. Portuguese India
Irian Barat West Iran
Island Iceland
Jubilé de l'Union Postale Switzerland
Kamerun Cameroons
Kaladlit Nunat, Kalaallit Nunaat Greenland
Karnten Carinthia
Karolinen Caroline Islands
KGCA Carinthia
Kgl. Post. Frim. Denmark, Danish West Indies
Khmere Cambodia
Kongeligt Post Frimaerke Denmark
KK Post Stempel Austria, Austrian Italy
KPHTH Crete
Kraljevina, Kraljevstvo Yugoslavia
Kreuzer Austria
KSA Saudi Arabia
K.u.K. Feldpost Austrian military stamps
K.u.K. Militärpost Bosnia and Herzegovina
K. Württ. Post Württemberg
La Canea Italian POs in Crete
La Georgie Georgia
Land-Post Baden
Lattaquie Latakia
Latvija Latvia

Turkey, 2003.

Canada, 1898.

Angola, 1990s.

Lietuvos Lithuania
Litwa Srodkowa Central Lithuania
Ljubljanska Pokrajina Slovenia
L. McL. Trinidad (Lady McLeod stamp)
Lösen Sweden
Magyar Hungary
MAPKA Russia
Marianen Mariana Islands
Maroc French Morocco
Marruecos Spanish Morocco
Marschall-Inseln Marshall Islands
Mejico Mexico
Militär Post Bosnia and Herzegovina
Mocambique Mozambique
Modonesi Modena
Montevideo Uruguay
Moyen-Congo Middle Congo
MViR German occupation of Romania
Nachmarke Austria
Napoletana Naples
NCE New Caledonia
Nederland Netherlands
Ned. Antillen Netherlands Antilles
Ned./Nederl. Indie Dutch East Indies
NF Nyasaland Field Force
Nippon Japan
Nieuwe Republiek New Republic (South Africa)
Norddeutscher Postbezirk North German Confederation
Norge, Noreg Norway
Nouvelle Calédonie New Caledonia
Nouvelles Hébrides New Hebrides

NSB Nossi-Be (Madagascar)
NSW New South Wales
NW Pacific Islands Nauru and New Guinea
NZ New Zealand
Oesterr., Oesterreich, Österreich Austria
Offentligt Sak Norway (official stamps)
Oltre Giuba Jubaland
Orts Post Switzerland
OS Norway (official stamps)
Ottoman, Ottomanes Turkey
P, PGS Perak (Government Service)
Pacchi Postale Italy (parcel stamps)
Pakke-Porto Greenland
Para Egypt, Serbia, Turkey, Crete
Parm[ensi] Parma
Pesa (on German) German POs in Turkey
Piaster German POs in Turkey
Pilipinas Philippines
Pingin Ireland
Poblact na hEireann Republic of Ireland
Poczta Polska Poland
Pohjois Inkeri North Ingermanland
Port Cantonal Switzerland (Geneva)
Porte de Conduccion Peru
Porte Franco Peru
Porte de Mar Mexico
Porteado Portugal and colonies
Porto Austria, Yugoslavia
Porto-pflichtige Württemberg
Post & Receipt/Post Stamp Hyderabad
Postage and Revenue United Kingdom

Postas le n'ioc Republic of Ireland
Postat e Qeverries Albania
Poste Estensi Modena
Poste Locale Switzerland
Postes (alone) Alsace and Lorraine, Belgium, Luxembourg
Poste Shqiptare Albania
Postgebiet Ob. Ost German Eastern Army
Postzegel Netherlands
Preussen Prussia
Provincie Modonesi Modena
Provinz Laibach Slovenia
PSNC Pacific Steam Navigation Co., Peru
Qeverries Albania
R Jind
Rayon Switzerland
Recargo Spain
Regno d'Italia Venezia Giulia, Trieste
Reichspost German Empire
RF France and colonies
RH Haiti
Repoblika Malagasy Malagasy Republic
Republica Oriental Uruguay
Répub. Franc. France
République Libanaise Lebanon
République Rwandaise Rwanda
Rialtas Sealadac na hEireann Provisional Government of Ireland
RO Eastern Roumelia
RSA Republic of South Africa
Rumanien (on German) German occupation of Romania
Russisch-Polen German occupation of Poland
Sachsen Saxony

Scrisorei Moldavia and Wallachia
Segnatasse Italy
Serbien Austrian or German occupation of Serbia
SH Schleswig-Holstein
SHS Yugoslavia
Shqipenia, Shqipenie, Shqypnija, Shqiptare Albania
Sld., Soldi Austrian Italy
Slesvig Schleswig
Slovensky Stat Slovakia
SO Eastern Silesia
SPM St Pierre and Miquelon
S. Thome e Principe St Thomas and Prince Islands
Suidwes Afrika South West Africa
Sul Bolletina, Sulla Ricevuta Italy
Sultunat d'Anjouan Anjouan
Suomi Finland
Sverige Sweden
SWA South West Africa
TAKCA Bulgaria
Tassa Gazzette Modena
Te Betalen Port Netherlands and colonies
TEO Cilicia. Syria
Terres Australes et Antarctiques Françaises French Southern and Antarctic Territories
Territoire Français des Afars et les Issas French Territory of the Afars and Issas
Tjanste Frimarke Sweden
Tjeneste Frimerke Norway
Tjeneste Frimaerke Denmark
Toga Tonga

Toscano Tuscany
UAE United Arab Emirates
UAR United Arab Republic (Egypt)
UG Uganda
UKTT United Kingdom Trust Territory (Southern Cameroons)
Uku Leta Hawaii
Ultramar Cuba. Porto Rico
UNEF Indian Forces in Gaza
UNTEA Western New Guinea
Vallées d'Andorre Andorra
Van Diemen's Land Tasmania
Venezia Giulia (on Italian stamps) Trieste
Venezia Tridentina Trentino
Viet Nam Dan Chu Cong Hoa North Vietnam
Vom Empfanger Einzuziehen Danzig (postage due)
YAR Yemen Arab Republic
YCCP Ukraine
YKP. H. P. Ukraine
Z Armenia
ZAR South African Republic (Transvaal)
Z. Afr. Republiek South African Republic (Transvaal)
Zeitungsmarke Austria, Germany (newspaper stamps)
Zil Eloine Sesel Seychelles Outer Islands
Zuid West Afrika South West Africa
Zulassungsmarke German military parcel stamp

Korea, 1995.

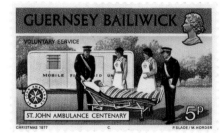

Republic of the Congo, 1990.   *Guernsey, 1977.*

GLOSSARY

Stamp collectors have a language all of their own, which can be puzzling to a newcomer. Some of the more commonly used terms are given below. References to glossed terms appear in bold.

Adhesive Stamp issued with **gum** on the reverse for sticking on mail, as opposed to one printed directly on the envelope, card or wrapper. *See also* Self-adhesive.

Aerogramme Specially printed air letter sheet on lightweight paper.

Airgraph World War II forces mail sent by micro-film, then enlarged for dispatch to the addressee.

Alphabets The different styles of lettering printed in the corners of British stamps 1840–87.

Backstamp Postmark on the back of an envelope, usually applied in transit or arrival.

Bantams South African stamps printed as a reduced format in World War II to save paper.

Bilingual pairs Stamps printed alternately in two different languages, as seen in issues from South Africa (1926–50) and Ceylon (1964).

Bisect Stamp cut in half for use at half the usual value, in times of shortage. Bisection may be made horizontally, vertically or diagonally.

Blind perforation Perforation in which the paper is merely dented, owing to blunt teeth in the perforating machine.

Block Four or more stamps joined together; also used in continental Europe as a synonym for a **miniature sheet**.

Bogus Label purporting to be a genuine stamp but without any validity or even a reason for issue other than to defraud collectors. Bogus overprints may be found on genuine stamps for the same reason.

Booklet One or more panes (small blocks) of stamps, usually held together with card covers.

Cachet Mark applied to cards and covers, other than the postmark, and often private or unofficial in nature.

Cancellation Postmark applied to stamps to prevent their re-use. Often hand- or machine-struck from steel or brass stamps, but may also be applied from a rubber, cork or wood stamp, or even by pen and ink.

Cancelled to order (CTO) Stamps postmarked in bulk, usually for sale to philatelists below face value; usually recognized by still having the gum on the backs.

Cantonals The earliest issues of Switzerland (e.g. Basle, Geneva and Zurich).

Carriers Stamps issued by private carriers, mainly in the United States, 1842–59.

Centred A stamp whose design is equidistant from the edges of the perforations is said to be well centred. Off-centre stamps have perforations (or scissor cuts if imperforate) cutting into the design on one or more sides.

Chalk-surfaced paper Security paper used for many British and colonial stamps to prevent re-use by cleaning off the cancellations. Can be detected by means of a silver pencil.

Chalky paper Special paper with a glossy surface used for many modern British definitive stamps, and also widely used for multicoloured stamps.

Chalon heads Name given to some early stamps of British colonies, e.g. Bahamas, Ceylon, New Zealand, Tasmania. reproducing a full-face portrait of Queen Victoria by Edward Chalon, RA.

Classics The earliest stamps of the world, 1840–1870.

Cliché Stereo or electro unit used in letterpress printing. These are assembled in a **forme** to form a printing plate.

Coils Stamps issued in reels or coils and often collected in **strips**. Can often be identified by being **imperforate** on two opposite sides.

Colour trials Impressions, or **proofs**, created in various colours prior to issue, for the purpose of determining the most suitable colours in actual production.

Combination cover Cover bearing stamps of two or more postal administrations, mainly from the early period when stamps had no franking validity beyond the frontiers of the country of issue.

Comb perforation Perforation on three sides of a stamp made at one stroke of the perforator, resulting in perfectly even corner teeth, compared with **line perforation**.

Commemorative A stamp sold in limited quantities for a period of time, often honouring a person, place, or event, but also used to promote certain current events.

Compulsory Stamp Charity stamps, issued at one time by countries such as Portugal and Yugoslavia, for compulsory use on mail.

Controls Letters and numerals found on British sheet margins, 1881–1947, for accounting purposes.

Cork cancellation Obliterators cut from corks, usually with fancy devices; widely used by 19th-century American postmasters. Also used in Britain to obliterate incorrect datestamps.

Corner block Stamps taken from the corner of a **sheet**, adjacent to marginal paper showing **controls**, **cylinder numbers**, plate numbers or printer's imprint.

Corner letters Double alphabet sequence of letters found in the corners of British stamps, 1840–87, indicating the position of the stamp in the **sheet**.

Cover Envelope or wrapper with stamps affixed or imprinted. Stamps are said to be "on cover" when the envelope is intact, as opposed to "on front" or "on piece".

CTO Widely used abbreviation for "**Cancelled to order**".

Cut to shape Imperforate stamps of unusual shapes, with margins trimmed accordingly.

Cylinder number Tiny numeral printed in the sheet margin to denote the cylinder(s) used in production.

Dandy roll Wire gauze cylinder used in the manufacture of paper and impregnation of **watermarks**.

Definitives Stamps in general use over a period of years, as opposed to **commemoratives**, charity or semi-postal stamps and other special issues.

Demonetized Obsolete stamps declared invalid for postage.

Die The original piece of metal on which the stamp design is engraved.

Die proof Impression pulled from the **die** to check its accuracy.

Dominical labels Small labels attached below Belgian stamps, 1893–1914, instructing the postmen not to

Uganda, 2000.

Luxembourg, 1944.

Gibraltar, 1970.

deliver the letter on Sunday. Where no objection was raised the labels were detached.

Dumb cancellation Postmarks with the town name erased for security reasons in wartime, and also special anonymous obliterations produced for the same purpose.

Engine-turning Intricate pattern of spiral lines forming the background to the earliest British and colonial stamps. This security device was copied from banknotes.

Entire Complete envelope, card or wrapper.

Entire letter Complete envelope or wrapper, with the original contents intact.

Embossed Stamps, or a portion of their design, die-struck in low relief, often colourless against a coloured background. Widely used for postal stationery.

Error Stamps deviating from the normal in some respect: missing or inverted colours, **surcharges** and **overprints** or mistakes in the design which may later be corrected. Usually worth more than normals, although in some cases (e.g. the Hammarskjold issue in the United States), the postal authority may take steps to minimize the rarity of the original.

Essay Preliminary design, not subsequently used.

Fake Genuine stamp that has been tampered with in some way to make it more valuable: e.g. fiscally used high-value stamps with the pen markings erased and a postmark substituted, or a stamp converted to a valuable rarity by the addition of an overprint.

First Day Cover or FDC Envelope bearing stamps used on the first day of issue.

First Flight Cover Cover carried on first airmail by a new route, or new aircraft.

Fiscal Stamp intended for fiscal or **revenue** purposes.

Flaw Defect in the printing **plate** or **cylinder**, resulting in a constant blemish on the same stamp in every sheet; plate flaws are useful in sheet reconstruction.

Forme Printer's term for the frame clamped around stereos or **clichés** to make a printing **plate** in the letterpress process.

Frank Mark or label indicating that a letter or card can be transmitted free of postage. Widely used by government departments. Military franks have been issued by France, Vietnam etc for use by personnel.

Gum Mucilage on the back of unused stamps. British stamps changed from gum arabic (glossy) to polyvinyl alcohol gum (matt, colourless) and later PVA Dextrin gum (with a greenish tint).

Gutter Area between panes of a sheet. Stamps from adjoining panes with the gutter between are known as gutter or interpanneau pairs.

Half tone Black-and-white photographic image appearing on a stamp; often a feature of early 20th-century **essays** where they were created by a simplified form of the photogravure process.

Healths Stamps issued by New Zealand since 1929 and Fiji (1951 and 1954), with a premium in aid of children's health camps.

Imperforate Stamps issued without any means of separating them, thus requiring them to be cut apart with scissors. Stamps with no perforations on one or more sides may come from **booklets** and those with no **perforations** on two opposite sides are from **coils**.

Imprint Inscription giving the name or trademark of the printer.

Imprint block Block of four or more stamps with marginal paper attached bearing the imprint.

Intaglio Printing process where the design is engraved in "recess", or below the surface of the printing plate.

Issue New stamp or stamps issued by a postal authority.

Jubilee line Line of printer's rule reinforcing the edges of the plate and first used on the British "Jubilee" series of 1887. Appears as bars of colour in the margin at the foot of the sheet.

Key plate Printing plate used to generate the design of the stamp. Used in conjunction with a duty plate, which prints the value.

Keytype Collectors' term for stamps of the British, French, German, Portuguese and Spanish colonies which used identical designs, differing only in the name of the colony and the denomination.

Kiloware Originally sealed kilogram bags of stamps on paper, but now applied to any mixtures sold by weight.

Line perforation Perforation where holes are punched out on one side of a stamp at a time, with the result that two sets of perforated lines do not register at the corners of the **sheet**.

Lithography Surface printing method where a design is photographically transferred to a zinc or aluminium **plate**. *See also* Offset lithography.

Locals Stamps whose validity is restricted to a single town or district and cannot be used for sending national or international mail.

Marginal markings Marks on the margins of sheets include **controls**, **cylinder numbers**, "traffic lights", printers' imprints, **jubilee lines**, sheet serial numbers, arrows showing the middle of the sheet, values of rows or sheets, ornament and even commercial advertising (France, Germany).

Meter marks Marks applied by a postage meter used by firms and other organizations. They comprise the indicium (or imitation "stamp" with the value), the town

Keytype die (with the date) and an advertising slogan, or may combine these elements in a single design. Invented in New Zealand (1904) and used internationally since 1922.

Miniature sheet Small sheet containing a single stamp or a small group of stamps, often with decorative margins.

Mint Unused stamp with full, original **gum** on the back.

Obsolete Stamp no longer on sale at the post office but still valid for postage.

Obliteration Post-marking of stamps to prevent re-use. *See also* cancellation.

Offset lithography Printing process whereby an image is transferred from an aluminum or zinc plate to a rubber blanket, and then from the rubber blanket to the paper.

Omnibus issue Commemoratives issued by several countries simultaneously, using similar designs.

Overprint Printing applied to a stamp some time after the original printing, to convert it to some other purpose (e.g. **commemorative**, charity, or for use overseas).

Pane Originally a portion of a **sheet** (half or quarter) divided by **gutters**, but also applied to the blocks of stamps issued in **booklets**.

Patriotics Covers and cards with patriotic motifs, fashionable during the American

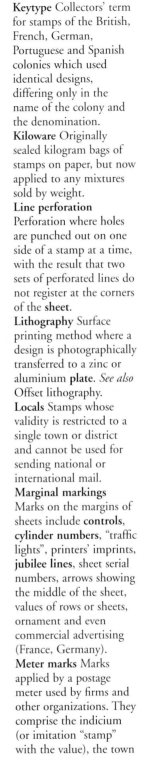

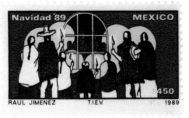

UK, 2002.   *Mexico, 1989.*   *Jamaica, 1966.*

Civil War, the Boer War and both World Wars.

Perfins Stamps perforated with initials or other devices as a security measure to prevent pilfering or misuse by office staff.

Perforation Form of separation using machines which punch out tiny circles of paper. *See also* Comb perforation; Line perforation.

Phosphor band Almost invisible line on the face of a stamp, created by the application of a chemical, to facilitate the electronic sorting process.

Photogravure Printing process where the design is photographed onto the printing **plate** using a fine screen which breaks the copy up into very fine square dots. The tiny depressions that form around the squares retain the ink.

Plate Flat or curved piece of metal from which stamps are printed.

Plate proof Impression of a **sheet**, **block** or **strip** of new issues, pulled from the **die**, usually in black ink, or sometimes in various colours.

Plebiscites Stamps issued in towns and districts, mainly after World War I, pending the vote of the population to decide which country they should join, e.g. Memel, Marienwerder, Carinthia and Silesia.

Postage dues Labels denoting the amount of postage unpaid or underpaid (often including a fine).

Postage paid

impressions (PPIs) Marks printed on envelopes, cards or wrappers, often used in bulk business mail.

Postal stationery Envelopes, cards and wrappers bearing **imprinted** or **embossed** stamps.

Pre-cancels Stamps used in bulk postings, with marks previously overprinted to prevent reuse. Widely used by Canada, Belgium, United States and France, but now largely superseded by **meter marks** and **postage paid impressions**.

Printer's waste Stamps with defective, double or misaligned printing, usually **imperforate**, and discarded during stamp production. Though usually strictly controlled, such material occasionally comes on to the market and is of interest to the specialist.

Proof Impression of a stamp design, pulled from the **die**. With perforated proofs, an overprint is often added to cancel the design and prevent it being used for postal purposes. *See also* Die proofs; Plate proofs.

Provisionals Stamps **overprinted** or **surcharged** to meet a shortage of regular issues. Also used by emergent nations pending a supply of distinctive stamps, the stamps of the former mother country being overprinted.

Recess printing Term used in catalogues to signify **intaglio** printing.

Re-entry Portion of an

intaglio plate which is re-engraved or re-entered by the transfer roller, usually detected by slight doubling of the lines.

Redrawn Stamps in which the basic design has been retained but various changes made in a subsequent edition.

Remainders Stocks of stamps on hand after an issue has been **demonetized** are sometimes sold off cheaply to the philatelic trade, with some form of cancellation to distinguish them from unused stamps sold at full value during the currency of the stamps.

Reprints Stamps printed from the original plates, sometimes long after the issue has ceased. They can be detected by differences in the paper, watermark and colour.

Retouch Repairs to letterpress plates and **photogravure** cylinders to touch out a flaw may result in stamps that can still be detected as slightly different from the normal. The corrected versions are known as retouches.

Revenue Stamp intended for **fiscal** or revenue purposes.

Rouletting Form of separation in which serrated instruments cut or pierce the paper without actually removing any, as in **perforation**.

Secret marks Tiny letters, numbers, dates and other devices introduced into the design of some stamps (notably the

United States and Canada) for security reasons.

Self-adhesive A stamp in a **coil** or **booklet** with backing paper from which it is peeled and affixed to mail without the necessity to lick or moisten the back.

Selvedge Stamp edging or sheet marginal paper.

Se-tenant Two or more stamps of different designs, values or colours, printed side by side.

Sheet A complete set of stamps taken from a single printing **plate**. This may then be cut into individual **panes** for sale at a post office.

Sheetlet Small sheet of stamps, of varying quantities depending the on country of issue.

Specimen Stamp perforated or overprinted thus, or its equivalent in other languages, for record or publicity purposes and having no postal validity.

Straight edge Stamps with no **perforations** on one or more sides, mainly found in **coils** and **booklets** but including **sheets** of stamps from countries such as Canada and the United States.

Strip Three or more stamps that have not been separated.

Surcharge An **overprint** that alters the face value of a stamp.

Tablet Adjoining section of a stamp that bears an inscription, advertisement or other design.

Tabs Stamps with marginal inscriptions alluding to the subjects

depicted, widely used by Israel and also by Switzerland and the United Nations.

Tied Postmarks that overlap the stamp and the envelope or card, a useful feature in establishing the genuineness of **bisects**.

Toughra (also tughra) Calligraphic markings indicating the signature of the former Sultan of Turkey, prevalent on Turkish issues predating the Ottoman Empire's demise in 1920.

Typography Collector's term for letterpress printing, abbreviated in catalogues to "typo".

Unused Stamp lacking a cancellation, but in less perfect condition than **mint**.

UPU Universal Postal Union.

Used Stamp bearing a cancellation.

Variety Any variation from the normal issue, relating to its shade, **perforation**, **watermark**, **gum** or phosphorescence, usually listed in the more specialized catalogues.

Vignette The main motif or central portion of a stamp design, as opposed to the frame, value **tablet** or inset portrait or effigy of the ruler.

Watermark Translucent impression used as a security device in the paper from which stamps are printed.

Zemstvos Russian local postal network which prepaid postage from the many smaller towns to the nearest imperial post office.

USA, 2003.

Italy, 1999.

Monaco, 1956.

INDEX

A

adhesive postage stamp, birth of 12–13
airmails 22–3, 54–5
  commercial airlines 71
  etiquettes 69
album weeds 56
albums, types 30–1, 32
  annotating pages 33
American Philatelic Society (APS) 80, 87, 88–9
American Poster Stamp Society 63, 89
American Topical Association 39, 86, 89
anniversaries 40
archives 88–9
army post offices (APOs) 52–3
arranging a collection 30–5
artwork 72
astrophilately *see* space
auctions 85, 87
  Mariazell Basilica 15
automatic machine stamps (ATMs) 18, 56

B

"back of book" stamps (BOB) 23
balloons 22, 54
Belgium 13
Bermuda 13
birth of adhesive postage stamp 12–13
bogus stamps 56, 57, 60, 61
bomb warnings, Israeli post 68
booklets 18
boundary changes 37
Bourke, John 78
Brazil 13
British Isles 16
  birth of adhesive postage stamp 12
  early services 11
  regional issues 36
British Philatelic Exhibition (BPE) 82
British Philatelic Trust (BPT) 58
Bull's Eyes 13
bureaux 85, 87
buying stamps 7, 84–5
  online 7, 87

C

Cambridge colleges' stamps 46, 71
cancellations 44, 45, 47
Cape of Good Hope Triangular 13, 16
carrier pigeons 55
carriers' stamps 70
catalogues 39, 56, 86, 88
  Scott 59, 70, 86, 88
  Stanley Gibbons 57, 79, 84, 88
certificate of posting 45
charity seals and labels 66–7
charity stamps 21, 71
children's charity labels 67
  ancient 10
Christmas seals 56, 66–7
church groups 71
Churchill, Winston 6, 41
Cinderella philately 56–7, 65, 68, 83, 89
circular delivery 70–1
city, as theme 43
clubs 7, 78, 79, 80, 81
coils 18
collateral material 34, 35, 43
collectors, early 78
colleges' stamps 46
comb perforations 14
commemoratives 20–1, 40
  labels 64–5
  Lewis and Clark 73
  Mariazell Basilica 15
competitive shows, entering 82–3
computers 35, 86–7
condition of stamp 84
congresses 81
contract remailing 71
conveying mail 11
country, collecting by 36–7
Crane's Chocolates poster stamp 64

D

datestamps 44, 51, 47
dealers 28, 79, 84–5
definitives 16–17, 20, 38
  postwar Germany 17
  United States 16–17
  see also Machins
De La Rue 66, 72, 73, 88
Denmark 17
deregulation 71
designing of stamps 72

detaching stamp from envelope 29
Diana, Princess of Wales 40
didactic stamps 42–3
die proofs 72
discussion forums, online 87
displaying stamps on the page 32–3
  advanced techniques 34–5
  computer-aided layouts 35
  thematics 38–9

E

Easter seals 67
  ancient 10
electronic sorting 14
Elizabeth II 40, 74, 83
  see also Machins
engraving 15, 72
entering competitive shows 82–3
envelopes, Mulready 19
errors, inverted Jenny 22
essays 72
etiquettes 69
Europa stamps 26, 39
events, as themes 40–1
exhibitions 80, 81, 82–3
  poster stamps 65
  Melbourne (1999) 58
Exposition Universelle, Paris (1900) 65

F

Fédération Internationale de Philatélie (FIP) 81, 83
field post offices (FPOs) in war 52
first day covers (FDCs) 27, 34, 62, 75, 81
fiscal stamps 68
fixed-leaf album 30
Flag Over Porch issue 14
flaws 75
  Wilding 2d 74
floating mail, St Kilda 58, 59
forgeries 56, 60–1
Frama company 18, 56
France 13
  pictorialism 38

G

Germany
  collecting range of 36
  Democratic Republic 17

Federal Republic 17
Reich 6
West Berlin 17
Gibbons, Stanley 79
  catalogues 57, 84, 88
government departments 19, 23
grade of stamp 84
Gray, Dr John Edward 78
Grimwood-Taylor, Pat 58
gum 14

H

Hawid strips 30, 31, 33
helicopter mail 55
Hill, Rowland 12, 19, 78
hingeless mounting system 31
Holboell, Einar 66
housing a collection 30–1

I

incidental philately 40–1
intaglio 15, 74
internet 35, 86–7
invasion post 53
Isle of Man 13, 43
  bomb warning post 68

K

Kennedy, John F. 41, 71
kiloware 29
Korea, charity labels 66

L

labels 12, 57
  American Civil War 57
  charity 66–7
  commemoratives 64–5
  parcel 46, 47, 69
  postage due 23
  postal services 57, 69
  poster stamps 64–5
  service indicator 57
  special treatment 69
laying out stamps 33
  advanced techniques 34–5
  computer-aided 35
  thematics 38–9
lettercards 19
letterpress 15, 72
Lewis and Clark commemorative 73
liberation stamps 53
line perforations 14
local philately 46–7

Germany, 1979.

Liechtenstein, 1982.

Gibraltar, 1970.

British Isles, 1937.

Finland, 1971.

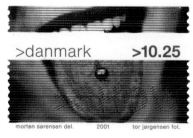

Denmark, 2001.